Chemically Dependent Women

Chemically Dependent Women

Assessment and Treatment

Josette Mondanaro, M.D.

Lexington Books

D.C. Heath and Company/Lexington, Massachusetts/Toronto

Library of Congress Cataloging-in-Publication Data

Mondanaro, Josette.
Chemically dependent women.

1. Substance abuse—Treatment.   2. Women—
Substance use.   3. Women—Mental health services—
Psychological aspects.   I. Title.
RC564.5.W65M66   1988   616.89′0088042   87–40428
ISBN 0–669–17235–9

Copyright © 1989 by Lexington Books

Published simultaneously in Canada
Printed in the United States of America
International Standard Book Number: 0–669–17235–9
Library of Congress Catalog Card Number: 87–40428

The paper used in this publication meets the minimum requirements of
American National Standard for Information Sciences—Permanence
of Paper for Printed Library Materials, ANSI Z39.48–1984.

88 89 90 91 92 8 7 6 5 4 3 2 1

Dedication

*To my mother and father, Alice and
Anthony, for giving me life, love, and
laughter.*

*To my precious son, Eden, for sharing with
me this life of love and laughter.*

To my lover, Giulia, for lighting my life.

Contents

Figures and Tables

Figures

Tables

Preface

Gloria Weissman
Community Research Branch
Division of Clinical Research
National Institute on Drug Abuse

In late 1985, the National Institute on Drug Abuse (NIDA) under-
took a new training initiative for service providers working with
drug abuse treatment clients. As part of this initiative, NIDA en-
visioned developing a training curriculum on current issues in the
treatment of chemically dependent women. Dr. Josette Mondanaro, an internationally respected expert in the field of alcohol and
drug treatment for women, was approached about the project and
agreed to undertake it for us.

Dr. Mondanaro, along with George Beschner of NIDA and
Beth Glover Reed of the University of Michigan, had edited two
NIDA volumes on treatment services for drug dependent women
during the early 1980s. Both of these books had been enthusiasti-
cally received by the field and continue to be in considerable demand, but it was clear that treatment providers needed information
about some new or newly recognized issues that had become very
important in the treatment of women, such as dual diagnosis, codependency, and AIDS prevention, as well as updated information
on areas such as cocaine, pregnancy and chemical dependency, and
benzodiazepine misuse.

Dr. Mondanaro developed the new training curriculum, with
assistance from Dr. Reed, and it was pilot tested in Washington,
D.C., during the spring of 1986. NIDA worked with state drug and
alcohol abuse agencies to set up a number of regional training
workshops. Dr. Mondanaro and Dr. Reed delivered the training in

Madison, Wisconsin; Tampa, Florida; Salt Lake City, Utah; and Kansas City, Missouri, during late 1986 and early 1987.

I was the NIDA project officer for those workshops and, as I listened to the questions and comments of participants, I was repeatedly impressed by how genuinely concerned treatment providers were with finding ways of bringing more women into treatment, keeping them in treatment, and dealing effectively with their special problems. Interest in the training and gratitude for the wealth of useful information it contained ran very high. We hoped that this project would continue so that Dr. Reed and Dr. Mondanaro could deliver the training to treatment providers and administrators throughout the country.

The growing epidemic of AIDS among IV drug abusers intervened, however, consuming much of NIDA's attention, as well as virtually all our funds for training. Dr. Mondanaro herself is now heading up an NIDA-funded AIDS prevention project working with the female sexual partners of IV drug abusers and with prostitutes. The project, called the Women and AIDS Risk Network (WARN), is active in three cities: Boston, Phoenix, and Los Angeles.

Certainly, AIDS and its relationship to drug use is a matter of great urgency. Yet, ironically, the AIDS epidemic has made the need for finding more effective ways of reaching and treating female drug abusers itself more urgent than ever. If we are to have an impact on behaviors of those women at greatest risk for this disease, we need to get them into treatment for their addiction and keep them there long enough to have a positive effect on their lives. We will not be able to do this unless our treatment programs become much more responsive to women. Even if we found a way to prevent and cure AIDS tomorrow, the other problems associated with alcohol and drug dependency would not disappear, and women would continue to suffer disproportionately from them because of inappropriate and inadequate treatment.

Because we at NIDA felt that Dr. Mondanaro's message was so important, we urged her to rework her training material into a book and seek a private publisher for it so that it could receive the widest possible distribution. We hope that, in this way, the work she did with us can continue and will be used to help those women who now need our help more than ever.

1
Chemically Dependent Women:
Outreach and Assessment

Chemical dependency now pervades American society, affecting individuals at every social and economic level, from the never-ending parade of actors and actresses treated at the Betty Ford Center to the street addicts who have become a permanent fixture of most of our cities. Chemically dependent women are among the most wounded and needy members of our society, yet their special problems have long gone underrecognized and undertreated. Women continue to be severely underrepresented in chemical dependency treatment programs, comprising only 19 percent of clients in federally funded alcohol treatment programs and 31 percent in federally funded drug treatment programs (NASADAD 1987).

Drug and alcohol treatment programs were designed initially by and for men. Programs admitted women as an afterthought, without regard for their particular needs. In fact, women were sometimes included primarily as objects onto which male clients could transfer their anger regarding mothers, wives, and girlfriends. Treatment designs included the breaking down of defenses through abrasive confrontational methods. Little thought or attention was paid to the fact that these techniques are countertherapeutic for most women and some men who are already extremely self-critical and have poorly developed boundaries.

Reed (1985) presents the following reasons why women continue to be underrepresented in drug and alcohol treatment programs:

- Admission criteria

- Lack of a gender-sensitive case-finding system

- Male-oriented treatment models

- Sexism and harassment within treatment programs

- Different help-seeking pattern of women compared to that of men

- Social stigmatization and/or social protection of drug and alcohol dependent women

- Family responsibilities

- Economic barriers

Indeed, there are characteristics of chemically dependent women, of society in general, and of drug programs in particular that lead to the underidentification and undertreatment of chemically dependent women. Attention to these three areas are necessary if we are to design more sensitive and effective interventions for chemically dependent women.

Attributes of Chemically Dependent Women

Psychological Factors

When compared with chemically dependent men or women who are not chemically dependent, chemically dependent women report lower levels of self-esteem, higher levels of depression, and higher levels of anxiety (Beschner, Reed, and Mondanaro 1981). The legacy of growing up female in a society that undervalues and denigrates the role of women is a low sense of self-esteem, high levels of depression and anxiety, and a sense of powerlessness. Learned helplessness is another result of the daily confrontation with the dominant culture. Women learn, through repeated negative reinforcement, that they are helpless to change their situation and thus see no alternative but to continue on their present path. All these characteristics act in concert to immobilize many chemically dependent women.

Employment and Education

Studies cited by Sutker (1981) demonstrate a level of unemployment in chemically dependent women that varies from 81 to 96 percent: Even after treatment, 72 percent of these women were still unemployed or lacking the skills necessary for gainful employment. Most chemically dependent women in federally funded treatment programs have not completed a high school education. Chemically dependent women also report lower incomes, poorer job histories, and less evidence of work-related identity (Reed 1981).

Children

Many studies report (Beschner, Reed and Mondanaro 1981) that a substantial proportion of chemically dependent women have children and that many more women than men entering treatment have the major caretaking and financial responsibility for their children. One study revealed that 60 to 70 percent of women in drug treatment had children. While women have greater family responsibilities than their male counterparts, they have fewer financial resources to meet them.

Addicted individuals in general appear to have more disturbances in their families of origin than people who are not chemically dependent. Chemically dependent women, however, report an even greater incidence of dysfunctional families than do chemically dependent men. According to Ryan (1980), women report more of the following in their families of origin: chemical dependency, mental illness, suicide, family violence, and physical and sexual abuse. In one study of two hundred chemically dependent families, it was found that 41 percent of the children were neglected or abused (Black and Mayer 1980).

Sexuality and Intimacy

Studies reveal a high rate of rape (46 percent) and incest (28 to 44 percent) among chemically dependent women (Mondanaro et al.

1982). These violent acts add to a woman's sense that she is not in control of her own life. In addition, anywhere from 58 to 84 percent of women express sexual concerns while in treatment. (See Mondanaro et al. 1982 for a detailed discussion of sexuality and intimacy in drug dependent women.)

Lesbians who seek treatment often encounter special problems.

> Numerous studies report that treatment programs often have a very difficult time in working with these clients. Part of the difficulty undoubtedly lies in some staff members' negative attitudes and lack of knowledge about the issues and biases that gay men and lesbians face. If staff are unable to separate sexual orientation issues from other aspects of gender role and identity and from problems arising from alcohol or drug use, they are likely to try to treat the lesbianism rather than the chemical dependency (Reed 1985, 27–28).

Lesbian and bisexual women might try to hide their sexual preferences to avoid anticipated hostility. For a detailed discussion of lesbians and drug treatment, see Mills and Nelson 1982.

Motivation for Changing Behavior

It has been learned that one's ability to use health education information and to make appropriate changes in one's behavior depends largely on socioeconomic status, level of education, sense of power, and vocation (Sandelowski, 1981). The chemically dependent woman is at an extreme disadvantage because of the compounding effects of low socioeconomic status, being female in a culture that undervalues the role of women, and often being a member of an ethnic minority. The lack of meaningful work, the problems of social isolation, and the presence of dysfunctional families make it difficult for such women to change their situation.

A low sense of self-esteem, coupled with depression, will have an immobilizing effect on women. Motivation is a reflection of self-esteem and depends on the belief that one is in control of one's life. Women often believe that they are controlled by their environment and that their actions will not result in positive changes. They also may believe that they do not have the ability to change.

Help-Seeking Behavior

Women do appear less likely than men to deny that they are experiencing problems. They become more self-critical than men once they realize that a problem exists and seek help sooner once they become self-critical.

The separate cultures of men and women are clearly reflected in their different help-seeking behaviors. It is congruent with gender stereotypes for women to be depressed and to seek help for mental health problems, but it is incongruent for them to be chemically dependent and to seek help with drug and alcohol problems. As a result, women are overrepresented in the mental health system and underrepresented in chemical dependency programs.

Women often identify problems related to their families, relationship with their partners, emotional difficulties (such as anxiety or depression), and medical well-being. They see their chemical dependency as a result of these other problems rather than as the primary problem and report the use of alcohol and drugs as a coping mechanism more often than do men. According to Reed (1985),

> More often, a woman will not even find her way into the chemical dependency treatment system initially. She may recognize that she is overusing a chemical; but she is much more likely to understand this as being related to some other event, most often a health, relationship, or mental health situation, or some other crisis. Thus while she is less likely to avoid the fact that a problem exists than a man would be, she is very likely to seek assistance from persons or systems that she perceives to have expertise in health, relationship, or mental health areas. (p. 36)

This is reflected in the fact that two-thirds of women alcoholics in Ontario are found in general service agencies rather than in drug or alcohol programs (Beckman and Amaro 1984).

Medical Illness/Physical Problems

Chemically dependent women appear to experience more medical complaints as a result of their alcohol and drug use than do chemically dependent men. Sixty-nine percent of women entering treatment cited physical health problems as the reason for entering drug treatment, as compared to 31 percent of the men. At intake, 75 percent of the women had medical complaints, as compared to 58 percent of the men (Mondanaro 1981).

Women appear to get sick more quickly with less liquor than men. Even when the difference in weight between men and women is adjusted, women do appear to have a special biological vulnerability to alcohol. The following table from Hill 1984 is a compilation of four studies conducted between 1972 and 1977. It depicts the dramatically higher mortality rates in women due to alcoholism. The figures reflect the ratio of observed to expected mortality among alcoholics.

	Male	*Female*
Circulatory disorders	2	5
Digestive disorders	4	5
Cirrhosis	8	23
Accidents	7	14
Suicide	11	16

It has been noted that women die earlier from cirrhosis than do men. In one study, the average age of women dying of cirrhosis was 48.6 years, as compared to 56.3 years for men. Women also show a much shorter average duration of excessive drinking before the first recorded occurrence of fatty liver, hypertension, obesity, anemia, malnutrition, gastrointestinal hemorrhage, and ulcers requiring surgery (Hill 1984).

When women present to their physicians with physical complaints, often neither they nor their physicians appreciate the role chemical dependency is playing in creating some of these symptoms. One study of physicians revealed that only 11 percent of women alcoholics presented with specific alcohol-identified problems. The other 89 percent presented with associated medical and emotional problems that were not properly linked with alcoholism (Beckman and Amaro 1984).

Most physicians are ill-prepared to deal with alcoholism and other drug dependencies. One sample of women members of Alcoholics Anonymous (AA) found that 50 percent of these women had tried to discuss their alcoholism with their physicians, only to be told that they could not possibly have an alcohol problem (Beckman and Amaro 1984).

Yet women, more than men, believe in the efficacy of medical treatment (Beckman and Amaro 1984). Unfortunately, when women do seek help from their physicians, they stand a good chance of having their chemical dependency overlooked and their underlying problems unappreciated and untreated. If a woman seeks medical help for her dysphoria, depression, and anxiety, she may be prescribed a tranquilizing medication; this removes a prime motivator for entering treatment. Although such medication might temporarily quiet the symptoms of anxiety, they do nothing to heal the underlying causes of the woman's distress. In addition, if she was initially experiencing difficulty with alcohol and other drugs, she will now become dually dependent and cross-addicted. The initial chemical dependency will progress as the woman takes her prescription psychoactive drugs. Years may go by before she finally receives the kind of assistance she needs. Chapter 5 provides a detailed discussion of the negative consequences of overprescribing tranquilizers to women.

Motivators for Treatment

While a woman is apt to seek some form of assistance once she realizes she has a problem, there is little in the typical woman's environment to confront her with the fact that she is experiencing difficulty with alcohol and/or other drugs. Most men become aware of and seek help for their chemical dependency problems through encouragement by their spouse, legal intervention (drunk driving arrests), or coercive intervention from work (Beckman and Amaro 1984). For most women, these points of potential intervention do not exist.

While chemically dependent men typically have non–drug using partners, chemically dependent women are likely to be alone or to have partners who are themselves chemically dependent. A chemically dependent partner will not be helpful in identifying the woman's drug problems or in motivating her to enter and complete treatment.

In a recent year in Santa Cruz County, California, only 11 percent of the two thousand people arrested for driving under the influence were women; this statistic reflects a nationwide trend. The explanations frequently cited for this are that women are often driven by someone else and that the stigma of alcoholism is seen as so great that law enforcement officials are loath to arrest women for this charge. In addition, women do drink alone more often than do men and are less likely to be out and about socializing.

A woman's work environment also often lacks the leverage needed to coerce her into treatment. It is unusual for a woman to be in a position of sufficient authority that her employer would see fit to pay for her chemical dependency treatment. More often, women work at jobs where there is no health insurance and where they can be easily replaced if their chemical dependency begins to affect their work performance.

The following table compares chemically dependent men and women in terms of who recommends treatment for them (Beckman and Amaro 1984).

Treatment Suggested By	Women	Men
Parents	41%	18%
Spouses	12%	46%
Children	31%	9%
Friends	25%	33%

Without intervention from work and the law, it is clear that "alcohol abuse has fewer social consequences, but more social stigma for women" (Beckman and Amaro 1984). This deadly combination keeps women out of appropriate treatment programs.

Women *do* respond if they feel that their chemical dependency is hurting their children (Beckman and Amaro 1984). Unfortunately, this is a double-edged sword. While the woman wants to get her life together for her children, she finds it difficult to separate herself from the day-to-day responsibilities of caring for them in order to go into treatment. Also, although children have the ability to affect a woman's perception of her problem, they typically do not have the ability or resources to assist her into treatment.

Barriers to the Treatment of Chemically Dependent Women

In addition to lacking the same kind of social motivators for treatment that men have, women often encounter more opposition to entering treatment than do men. Beckman and Amaro (1984) reported that 23 percent of the women entering treatment experienced opposition from their families and friends, as compared to only 2 percent of the men. In addition, 48 percent of the women experienced problems due to entering treatment, as compared to 20 percent of the men.

The following list, presented by Reed (1985), summarizes many of the barriers to treatment already discussed, plus several others. It is divided into three components: factors that might prevent women from seeking and entering treatment; factors that are likely to be problematic in the early stages of treatment; and factors posing barriers to long-term recovery.

Barriers to Treatment Entry

- Lack of economic resources
- Child-related responsibilities
- Lack of women-oriented services
- Less sensitive referral network

   Stigma/stereotypes
   Lack of knowledge
   No case-finding systems in places women typically seek help

- Lack of interpersonal network support
- Women attend to others' needs more than their own

Barriers to Engagement in Treatment

- Low self-esteem

- Too many other responsibilities
- Lack of a comprehensive assessment
- Sexism

  Stereotypes, insensitivity
  Demeaning roles
  Sexual harassment

- Inadequate sensitivity to gender-related interpersonal and group dynamics

  Gender of intake worker/counselor
  Styles of early treatment stages (for example, confrontation)
  Groups and organizational gender composition and dynamics

Barriers to Sobriety/Abstinence/Improved Quality of Life

- All barriers in the preceding categories
- Lack of available, sensitive self-help groups
- Lack of meaningful roles; underemployment
- Financial difficulties
- "Other" orientation
- Nonconscious ideology
- Lack of assertiveness and skills for autonomous living
- Other psychiatric disorders
- Unresolved intimacy/sexuality/body image issues (often related to incest or assault)

Increasing Women's Participation in Drug and Alcohol Treatment

Understanding the gender issues, the help-seeking behavior of women, and the barriers to treatment for women is the first step in designing a program that will be attractive and responsive to them. Such a program should include an outreach branch that can respond to the special problems and characteristics that distinguish female from male drug abusers.

Reaching the Women

One important but often overlooked way of reaching women is through direct appeals to the women themselves. Women are more responsive to advertising, publicity, and other outreach activities than men (Beckman and Amaro 1984). Aggressive educational and informational activities will go far in reaching women. An effective program of community education should include the following elements.

Disease Concept. More women will seek help when the public understands that chemical dependency is a treatable disease. These women are sick trying to get well, not bad trying to be good. For the most part, society still equates chemical dependency with moral weakness. Widespread dissemination of the disease concept of this illness will assist women in being identified and helped into treatment by their families and friends.

There has been some confusion about the terms *disease concept* and *medical model*. The disease concept refers to the growing body of knowledge demonstrating that chemical dependency, especially alcoholism, is in part genetically and biochemically determined. This should not be confused with what has been termed the medical model. While the disease concept speaks to the origin of chemical dependency, the medical model refers to one component of chemical dependency treatment. Accepting the disease concept does not mean believing that all chemically dependent individuals need in-hospital treatment.

Efficacy of Treatment. Many people believe not only that chemically dependent individuals are morally weak, but also that treatment does not work. The public needs to be educated about the treatment of this disease, the concepts of abstinence and sobriety, and the hopefulness involved in a recovery program. More women will identify themselves as chemically dependent when negative views about chemical dependency are reduced, and more women will seek appropriate treatment when they understand that their disease is eminently treatable.

Utilizing Current Publicity and Trends. By heightening awareness of some problems, the media can provide an exquisite opportunity for treatment programs for chemically dependent women. For example, Robin Norwood's best-selling book *Women Who Love Too Much* has introduced millions of women to the concept of codependency. After reading this book, many women will no doubt seek treatment for "loving too much." Treatment programs can take advantage of this trend by offering special groups for these women. Often women who are codependent are also chemically dependent, but find it more acceptable to enter treatment for codependency. Their chemical dependency can then be approached through interventions for codependency. Distorted body image and eating disorders also have been the subject of much media attention. Some eating disorders have been linked to chemical dependency, and a treatment program that offers assistance for women with eating disorders will attract a large number of chemically dependent women. A similar situation occurs with adult children of alcoholics. Individuals, especially women, might be more willing to identify themselves as adult children and to seek help for this problem than to seek help for their own chemical dependency.

Agoraphobia is another disease that has received much media attention and is closely associated with chemical dependency. Offering treatment for women who suffer from this disease is another way of attracting women who would otherwise not identify themselves as chemically dependent. As is discussed in chapter 6, both disorders must eventually be addressed in other for treatment to be effective.

Treatment programs should be prepared to meet chemically dependent women on their own ground. Clearly, dealing with substance dependency will precede recovery in other areas, but attention must be given to the dis-ease that brought the woman into treatment in the first place.

Reaching the Gatekeepers

To reach women, it is important to enhance awareness of and services for chemical dependency among the providers from whom women seek help. These gatekeepers for chemically dependent women include battered women's shelters, physicians (family doctors, gynecologists, and pediatricians), emergency rooms, women's crisis centers, mental health agencies, family and parenting programs, child protective services, clergy, beauticians, child-care professionals and school staff, pharmacists, and civil or divorce attorneys.

Reed (1985) found that outreach programs in emergency rooms have been effective in identifying and referring drug dependent women who have never received treatment for their chemical dependency. Recognizing that women typically perceive chemical dependency as triggered by other life events and seek assistance for those other problems, the California state government placed drug treatment funds into existing women's crisis programs, including battered women's shelters, programs for widows, feminist counseling centers, mothers' emergency stress services, rape counseling centers, and employment programs. Soler and Dammann (1981) found that of the 5,129 women who entered these programs in a twenty-month period, 39.4 percent identified themselves as dependent on alcohol and/or other drugs. In addition, the rate of sedative, tranquilizer, and/or amphetamine use was almost twice that of a stratified national survey population. Finally, more than 50 percent of those who listed tranquilizers, barbiturates, or sedative/hypnotics as their primary drug used this drug on a daily or more frequent basis.

These programs knew how to provide services to women. What they did not know was how to treat chemical dependency. This particular grant allowed these competent and capable programs to enhance their skills in chemical dependency. Indeed, it is cost effective to train existing women's resources to identify and treat chemical dependency. In addition, it might be more effective for the woman client to be treated within a setting that fits the way she has identified her problems and her help-seeking behavior.

Program Design

To attract and keep women clients, the treatment program must be designed to meet their special needs. Although this information has been available for more than a decade, programs have been slow to create responsive atmospheres and services. Most programs cannot afford to provide all these services directly, but they can ensure their availability through formal arrangements with other service providers. (See Kovach 1981 for methods of identifying and developing referral linkages.) "Availability means not only that services exist but they are willing and able to serve chemically dependent women sensitively and effectively" (Reed 1985). Based on and adapted from Reed's recommendations, core services for women should include the following:

1. Medical/health

   a. Diagnosis and treatment of medical problems

   b. Gynecological services

   c. Psychiatric assessment

   d. Health promotion (including nutrition planning, physical fitness activities, and education about how to interact assertively with the health-care system)

   e. Treatment for prescription drug dependency (including detoxification services)

   f. Work on issues related to body image, overeating, and eating disorders

   g. Pregnancy-related services

2. Child-related

   a. Child care (either on-site or via referral arrangement)

   b. Services to children (minimally, assessment and referral; ideally, educational sessions and children's groups)

   c. Parenting education

3. Family services
   (For significant others and the family as a whole; the program must be careful not to define *family* too narrowly and to involve those important to the client, whatever their official relationships.)

    a. Family wellness education (how to survive as a happy family)

    b. Relationship counseling

    c. Referral or counseling concerning codependency

4. Vocational

    a. Job readiness training

    b. Vocational skill training

    c. Job-seeking support and coaching

5. Skill training to develop self-esteem and coping

    a. Assertiveness training

    b. Financial management education

    c. Instruction in personal goal setting

    d. Education in stress and crisis management

    e. Assistance in developing communication skills and a support system

    f. Discussion of gender and socialization issues

    g. Instruction in basic survival skills

6. Chemical dependency education

    a. Education about the physical, social, and family consequences of the disease of chemical dependency

    b. Preparation for engaging in self-help groups such as Alcoholics Anonymous, Narcotics Anonymous, AL-ANON, and Women for Sobriety

7. Legal assistance

    a. Help with whatever criminal issues exist

    b. Assistance with the more common civil matters such as child custody, landlord disputes, and divorce or separation

8. Sexuality and intimacy

   a. Discussions and interventions concerning incest and rape

   b. Education about sexuality and drugs

   c. Counseling about fear of intimacy

   d. Use of outside support groups such as Daughters Anonymous for incest survivors

9. Women who love too much

   a. Education concerning adult children of alcoholics, codependency, and women who love too much

   b. Referral to appropriate reading material and support groups

Assessment and Treatment Planning

Bringing women into treatment is only the first step; keeping them there and providing truly effective treatment might be far more difficult. Assessment and treatment planning for women ought to include all the service areas delineated in the core list above.

The following chapters discuss in detail some of the current needs of chemically dependent women. Through more thoughtful attention to and appreciation of the unique needs of women, treatment programs and therapists will be able to design more successful strategies for the prevention, early intervention, and treatment of chemical dependency in women.

2
The Ultimate in Female Socialization

Women Who Love Too Much, Codependents, and Adult Children of Chemically Dependent Parents

Over the past five years, there has been a growing awareness of the particular problems associated with being the partner or the child of an individual with a chemical dependency. Although the bulk of the research and literature in this area deals with the disease of alcoholism, the issues raised are equally relevant to families that are involved with other drugs.

In the past it was believed that an individual was codependent by virtue of having an alcohol or drug dependent partner; that is, the partner's disease of chemical dependency gave the individual the title and role of codependent. Now, however, we are beginning to appreciate that an individual who is codependent has a disease that is separate from her or his partner's chemical dependency and that a codependent has certain personality traits that are present even without a chemically dependent partner. These characteristics and traits are what lead the codependent to select partners who are either chemically dependent or dysfunctional, and hence unavailable, in other ways.

It must be stressed that this newer definition of the term *codependent* represents a real departure from the more traditional view. In the past, codependents were seen as people (most frequently women) who were available to assist in the recovery of a chemically dependent person. While AL-ANON recognizes that the codependent needs her or his own recovery program, this newer concept goes farther by saying that the codependent has a series of characteristics that preceded her or his involvement with the chemically dependent person and would be there whether or not she or he selected such a partner.

Frequently, chemically dependent women have partners who are also chemically dependent. In addition to being codependent, many chemically dependent women were raised in chemically dependent families. We are now beginning to appreciate the deep and lasting effects of growing up in such families. Current treatment programs use the acronym ACA or ACOA (adult children of alcoholics) to describe adults who have been raised in families addicted to alcohol. In this chapter, *ACA* or *adult child* will refer to the broader category of adults raised in any chemically dependent family.

Codependents, adult children of chemically dependent families, and women who love too much all have the same characteristics. Not believing that they are capable of being loved, they settle for being needed. There is a powerful sense that if they work hard enough and long enough and just love someone else well enough, they will be loved in return. This is a very long and indirect route to being loved, and most of these women rarely find the love they are seeking because they are looking in the wrong places.

Since these women need to be needed, they are attracted to men or women who are particularly needy. They see the potential in their partners and often believe that they can fix the partner. These women are attracted to the pathos in others and believe that their love and attention will heal their partners' wounds, which will allow their partners to love them.

Socialized to be adaptive and responsive to the needs of others and trained to derive satisfaction from making others happy, all women are capable of becoming women who love too much. Codependents, adult children of chemically dependent parents, and women who love too much all share the common characteristics of loving until it hurts, selecting needy and emotionally unavailable partners, and hoping that they will be loved once they fix their partners. On a bell-shaped curve, it can be seen that women who allow themselves to be physically abused are at the extreme end of loving until it hurts.

This chapter presents the current thinking regarding codependency and adult children and integrates these findings with relevant information emerging from the fields of mental health and developmental psychology.

The Family of Origin

The chemically dependent family is characterized by chaos, unpredictability, and inconsistency. Children in these families learn early to expect the unexpected. The family's central organizing principle is to maintain the secrecy surrounding both the chemical dependency and its deleterious effects. This is poignantly reflected in the following statement by an adult child: "In our family there were two very clear rules: The first was that there is nothing wrong here, and the second was, don't tell anyone" (Beletsis and Brown 1981, 6).

It is not just that these children are responding to the chaos caused by the presence of the drug, the need to maintain the family secret, the denial, and the constant failure to control the uncontrollable. These children also have not received mirroring, respect, sympathy, understanding, and echoing. Their own feelings have not been made real by the essential validation of their parents. They learn to reflect their parents' feelings and to anticipate their parents' needs while their own feelings go unappreciated by both themselves and their parents. Soon these children go beyond denying the feelings and become unable to experience their own feelings. Instead of experiencing what they want or feel, the children experience what they believe the parents want them to feel.

These children grow into adults who do not know what they are feeling unless they can respond to the needs of others. One such client in my practice was absolutely lost in role playing. She did not know what to say or do when confronted with only herself. In family sessions, she could respond to her parents only by doing what they wanted her to do or by rebelling against them and doing what they did not want her to do. She was still unable to connect with what she wanted to do and to identify what she was feeling.

Developmental Wounds

The deep wounds these children have experienced in the deprived environment of the drug dependent or alcoholic family affect fundamental requirements for healthy development identified by a number of theorists. D.W. Winnicott, Margaret Mahler, and Heinz Kohut have stated that "[t]he child has a primary need to be regarded and respected as the person he really is at any given time, and as the central actor in his own activity. . . . Children need the presence of a person who is completely aware of them and takes them seriously, who admires and follows them" (Miller 1981, 7).

The child in a drug dependent family is raised without respect and tolerance for his or her feelings. The parents do not see the child as the center of his or her own activity, but rather as an extension of themselves. In the drug dependent family, the drug becomes the central actor around which all family activities and interactions revolve. The child learns quickly to perceive and respond to the needs of the parents. The child receives love by anticipating the needs of others; thus being needed replaces or becomes synonymous with being loved. As time passes, the child takes on more and more responsibility—in the home, for other siblings, and in school—in an attempt to control the uncontrollable. "In everything they undertake they do well and often excellently; they are admired and envied; they are successful whenever they care to be— but all to no avail. Behind all this lurks depression, the feeling of emptiness and self-alienation, and a sense that their life has no meaning" (Miller 1981, 6).

These children lack an appreciation and understanding of their own inner emotional world, a world that is characterized by a lack of respect, a compulsion to control, manipulation, and a demand for achievement (Miller 1981).

False Self

To satisfy the parents' needs, the child sacrifices her or his own true self. Winnicott has said that constantly accommodating the parents' needs causes the child to develop a false self. The child has acted as if there were no discrepancies between what was expected and what she or he was actually experiencing. The true self is in a state of noncommunication to the point that "the child does not know what he is hiding" (Miller 1981, 15). "The true self cannot communicate because it has remained unconscious, and therefore undeveloped, in its inner prison" (Miller 1981, 21).

The outward appearance of this child (the false self) is dramatically different from the way the child experiences herself or himself. Excellent school performance, mature personality, and responsible outward behavior all belie the child's inner feelings of inadequacy, failure, depression, emptiness, and impotence. Miller (1981) captures the agony of the child locked in the adult when she says:

> In analysis, the small lonely child that is hidden behind his achievements wakes up and asks: "What would have happened if I had appeared before you, bad, ugly, angry, jealous, lazy, dirty, smelly? Where would your love have been then? And I was all these things as well. Does this mean that it was not really me whom you loved, but only what I pretended to be: the well-behaved, reliable, empathic, understanding, and convenient child, who in fact was never a child at all? What became of my childhood? Have I not been cheated out of it? I can never return to it. I can never make up for it. From the beginning I have been a little adult. My abilities—were they simply misused?" (Miller, p. 15)

Boundary Confusion

If the mother is chemically dependent, basic nurturing and care giving may be severely impaired. If the father is chemically dependent, the mother's attention may be focused on his addiction and not on the child. In either case, the child's needs come second to the drug. The father may have a relationship with the chemical, and the mother may develop an insidiously incestuous relationship with the child to fill the vacuum in the marital dyad. In this situation there is not the obvious physical incest, but an inappropriate and dysfunctional emotional attachment. The child will then suffer the double injury of not being seen and responded to as a needy child and then being inappropriately elevated to the level of a confidante and partner. (See Mondanaro et al. 1982 for a discussion of this topic.)

This role reversal and boundary confusion leads to the development of an external locus of control; that is, the individual comes to believe that she or he is not in control of her or his emotions but that these feelings are controlled by the actions of others. In addition, the child's ability to construct a defined self is severely impaired.

Control

Control is a central dynamic as the child tries to manage the actions of the chemically dependent adults. The child might feel important or even omnipotent as she or he attempts to have an effect, but these attempts typically meet with failure because she or he is trying to control something that is intrinsically beyond her or his control. This desire to control continues into adulthood.

> Doing alright means keeping things under control. Keeping things under control often means doing it perfectly, satisfying the boss completely, or having interpersonal relationships in which feelings are hidden and all goes smoothly. ACA's often take on, or experience, an enormous amount of responsibility in all areas of their lives. They have trouble sharing responsibility, feeling this as a loss of control. No matter how well they do, it is never quite enough. (Beletsis and Brown 1981, 14)

Survival Mechanisms

The survival mechanisms employed by the child include denial, withdrawal, lack of trust, secrecy, overcontrol of self, adaptation, and control of the environment. Yet the very defenses that allow the child to survive and function in this environment are the mechanisms that create the dysfunctional patterns in adulthood. These adult difficulties include problems with interpersonal relationships, an inability to tolerate intimacy, unsuccessful differentiation from parent, and an inability to develop confidence (Beletsis and Brown 1981). Perhaps the single most serious consequence of the child's early adaptation to the parents' needs is "the impossibility of consciously experiencing certain feelings of his own such as jealousy, envy, anger, loneliness, impotence, anxiety either in childhood or later in adulthood" (Miller 1981, 9).

Choice of Partner: Compulsion to Repeat

Partner choice is closely related to the characteristics of the mother or father, referred to as the primary object. To show dissatisfaction with the primary object is to risk the loss of the mother or father. Therefore, the child and the child locked in the adult have a compulsion to repeat and reenact the primary relationship. It is a familiar role, one that the child has experienced for years. "The fascination of tormenting relationships is part of the compulsion constantly to reenact one's earliest disappointments with one's parents" (Miller 1981, 83).

The female child who has not been loved enough becomes the woman who loves too much. The care-giving instincts of these adults respond instinctively to the neediness in others. They believe that if they just work hard enough, are good enough, and suffer enough, they will be able to change their needy partner into someone who will ultimately give them love. Besides the safety afforded by the familiarity of this role, there is also the challenge of reenacting the family script but altering the ending. There is a sense that this time will be different, this time the adult child will succeed in fixing the partner and finally win the love she has been craving. According to Norwood (1985), "It is this thrilling possibility of righting old wrongs, winning lost love, and gaining withheld approval that, for women who love too much, is the unconscious chemistry behind falling in love" (p. 103).

The compulsion to repeat will continue until the individual becomes involved in a treatment process. "That probably the greatest of narcissistic wounds—not to have been loved just as one truly was—cannot heal without the work of mourning. It can either be more or less successfully resisted and covered up (as in grandiosity and depression), or constantly torn open again in the compulsion to repeat" (Miller 1981, 85).

Selecting needy partners is also a way for such women to maintain rigid denial about their own pains and needs. Controlling the outer environment assists them in maintaining control over their inner selves. These women are exquisitely tuned in to the needs of others. Their satellite dishes are aimed outward, vigilantly scanning the horizon and picking up on the needs of others. What is missing is a second satellite dish that should be turned inward, scanning their internal territory, focusing on their needs, feelings, and desires.

This information sheds new light on the concept of codependency. One is not codependent because one has a drug or alcohol dependent partner but because of the way one has been raised both by one's parents and by this culture. Codependency is a distinct entity separate and apart from chemical dependency. A codependent would be a codependent whether or not she had a drug or alcohol dependent partner.

Cultural Influences
on Adult Children and Codependents

It has been reported that 90 percent of the adult children seeking treatment are women and that the overwhelming majority of codependents also are women. Some attribute this to the fact that women find it easier to seek help for mental health–related problems than do men, but other factors might be involved as well. For example girls in this culture are raised to be dependent, care giving, nurturing, and other-directed. They are taught to anticipate and respond to the needs of others. It may be hypothesized that girls, more often than boys, are given the responsible role in the drug dependent family because this role is already closely aligned with the familial and cultural expectations for them. Girls in drug dependent families thus receive a double dose of the message that they are supposed to respond to the needs of others; they receive this message both from society and from their families. No cognitive dissonance is created for the girl raised in this environment. Alternatively, if a boy were to be selected as the responsible child in a drug dependent family, he would experience some dissonance since society at large is grooming him for a very different role. The drug dependent family can thus be seen as a particularly toxic environment for girls.

Adult Children and Chemical Dependency

Children of alcohol and drug dependent parents are at a greater biological risk for developing the disease of chemical dependency. Besides the biochemical/genetic influences, there also exists a psychological pull toward addiction. As stated by one client in a group for adult children, "To become an alcoholic is one way of not being different, of not betraying or deserting the family. It is the one clear way to belong: drinking validates my membership in my family" (Brown and Beletsis 1986, 11).

It appears that a large proportion of adult children are either actively drug dependent or expend a tremendous effort to control their alcohol and drug use. The bind these individuals experience is reflected in the following observation: "To stop drinking was to reject an identification with his father. To keep drinking was to risk being an alcoholic without choices and was rejection of his mother" (Brown and Beletsis 1986, 12). To demonstrate that they are different from both parents, adult children often try extremely hard to control their drinking and drug use. If they can control their drug use, they can prove that they did not suffer from their parents' disease.

Separation

Ill-prepared to venture out into the adult world, many adult children take refuge in maintaining an overinvolvement with the family of origin. Even if they have moved out physically, they still feel excessively connected and responsible. Within this familiar setting, the adult child can bolster her or his sense of self-esteem by once again repeating the role she or he knows so well. These individuals are still trying to fix the family, especially if there are younger siblings at home (Beletsis and Brown 1981).

This has serious implications for treatment. "Since their only sense of self-worth has come from what they have done for the family, the unconscious decision to begin the separation process and to begin relinquishing responsibility for the alcoholic activates intense anxiety and can be experienced not only as a major loss, but a loss of control and a loss of meaning in their lives as well" (Beletsis and Brown 1981, 23). To be a member of the family, the individual must maintain the denial and hold the same values and beliefs as other family members. The decision to seek treatment for being an adult child is to make real the past. This is a monumental step. The individual is letting go of "a lifelong major family secret: a secret that still binds many to their families" (Brown and Beletsis 1986, 3). The adult child must make a leap of faith. She or he must let go of her or his identity with the family of origin before being able to learn how to trust others and to develop healthy intimate relationships.

The strenuousness of this task is reflected by the fears expressed by the participants in a group for adult children: "If I trust you it is like giving a piece of myself to you. And I don't know what you will do with it." "I had the fantasy that when I came back to the group no one would be here" (Beletsis and Brown 1981, 25).

Therapeutic Process

Many models for the treatment of adult children and codependents are being explored. Perhaps what is most important is a solid understanding of how these individuals have been wounded and an appreciation for the in-depth work necessary for the healing process to occur.

Long-Term Interactional Group Therapy

Long-term group therapy has been used at the Stanford Alcohol Clinic for the past eight years. Each six-member group meets for ninety minutes weekly with two coleaders. The average length of participation is three years. The groups concentrate on the process of family transference. Participants "view the group as the family of origin and behave in the group as one once did in that first family" (Brown and Beletsis 1986, 98). Within the context of this group, adult children learn to grow up, grow out, and come home.

In the early stages of the group, the individuals work on concepts of denial (personal and familial), belonging, and what it means to be chemically dependent. It is difficult for adult children to tolerate differences among themselves. "For adult children of alcoholics to be different is to risk rejection and separation. To be close and depend on the group touches anxiety about loss" (Brown and Beletsis 1986, 100).

Group participation is also made difficult by the fact that these individuals survived their childhood precisely by not needing anyone. It is especially difficult for the participants to accept the limits of their abilities to help others and to fix situations that are not theirs to fix.

They are being asked to do two extremely difficult tasks: bond to the group and return to their childhood. "The idea of experiencing oneself as a child is not tolerable to all members. . . . For many, being a child carried nothing but fear and feelings of helplessness. It was better to grow up fast. The promise of regression is experienced as a terrifying loss of control" (Brown and Beletsis 1986, 6).

Over time the group members explore the intricacies of the following concepts (Brown and Beletsis 1986):

- Their relationships with each other
- Trust
- Commitment and intimacy
- The nature of appropriate responsibility to each other
- Tolerance for differentness

- Autonomy
- Their inability to control others

In the process of growing up, the participants break through their denial of the past, regress, and experience themselves as children through family transference in the group. They learn to detach and separate from the chemically dependent family. They learn that they cannot fix the family and that they must now focus on themselves. After detachment and separation, participants learn to go home, but in a very different way. No longer will they participate in the family secret. No longer will they try to control that which they cannot control. "The process of reinterpreting the past as it is repeated in the present context of the group, relinquishing fantasies of omnipotence as well as impotence, and integrating insight and experience in a way that permits effective interpersonal relationships are the rewards of the difficult and painful work done in the ACA group" (Brown and Beletsis 1986, 28).

AL-ANON and Other Self Help Groups

Perhaps one of the biggest boosts to AL-ANON has been Robin Norwood's book *Women Who Love Too Much*. This book translates the core concepts of AL-ANON and codependency into an understandable format for millions of people. The promise of recovery is clear: "You will change from a woman who loves someone else so much it hurts into a woman who loves herself enough to stop the pain" (Norwood 1985, preface).

In outlining the steps to recovery, Norwood states:

It seems so much easier and feels much more familiar to keep on looking for a source of happiness outside oneself than to practice the discipline required to build one's inner resources, to learn to fill the emptiness from inside rather than outside. But for those of you who are wise enough, weary enough, or desperate enough to want to get well more than you want to either fix the man you are with or find a new one—for those of you who really do want to change yourself, the steps of recovery follow. (p. 219)

The steps suggested by Norwood reflect the AL-ANON program:

1. Go for help
2. Make your own recovery the first priority in your life
3. Find a support group of peers who understand
4. Develop your spiritual side through daily practice
5. Stop managing and controlling others
6. Learn to not get "hooked" into games
7. Courageously face your own problems and short-comings
8. Cultivate whatever needs to be developed in yourself
9. Become "selfish"
10. Share with others what you have experienced and learned (pp. 221–22)

While Norwood's book speaks about women who love men too much, this situation is not particularly different for women who love women too much. It is imperative that treatment programs acknowledge the existence of lesbian relationships and make room for codependent lesbians to engage in the recovery process.

A Word of Caution

Many programs and counselors, inspired by the detailing of a paradigm that explains the pain experienced by so many individuals, are establishing interventions for the adult child, the codependent individual, and women who love too much. Unfortunately, many of these interventions fail to grasp the depth of the developmental traumas experienced by these individuals. Treatment approaches that offer an ACA group for eight weekly sessions do not reflect the long-term work that is necessary to help the adult child develop an internal structure. Eight-week groups or two-day seminars can educate people to the problem but do not constitute therapy.

Failure to appreciate the depth of the wounds and the rigorous therapeutic process needed for a successful intervention lead programs, writers, and counselors to design interventions that are at best superficial and at worst harmful. Adult children, seeking perfection and to make themselves more presentable by adaptation, will be drawn to any program or process that promises a quick fix. Unfortunately, these books and groups often fail to engage the individual in a deep therapeutic alliance. Rather they serve to reinforce the adult child's need to "do it better." Thus intervention might tap into the disease process of the false-exterior self rather than the recovery process.

This is evidenced by the ever-growing number of adult children who have read the books and gone to the eight-week groups or seminars, and now are wondering why they are not better. One such woman related her feelings when she called for an individual therapy appointment. The relief she had initially felt when she read about adult children led to an enthusiastic involvement with a short-term group. Her relief and enthusiasm ultimately gave way to a deep depression: "I've read the books, understand the problem, and have gone to treatment, so why do I still feel so bad?"

Adult children are good students. This woman was able to utilize her highly developed external false self and act as if she was changing her behavior. Unfortunately the deeper, underlying wounds went undetected and untreated. Treatment programs aided the progression of her disease by offering a superficial approach to a deeply rooted problem.

Perhaps counselors and some writers in this field are negatively affected by their own history as adult children. Being perfectionists who are driven to appear capable and competent, they might have tried to progress too quickly in their own recovery process. Perhaps they did not allow themselves enough time to be the client before they moved into becoming the therapist trying to assist other recovering adult children.

It would be unfortunate for this newly developing field to become tied to treatment approaches that may, in part, reflect the very processes that constitute the disorder. Integrating work from developmental theorists and clinicians such as D.W. Winnicott, Margaret Mahler, Heinz Kohut, and Alice Miller will enable therapists to better understand the nature and extent of these wounds and will facilitate more effective interventions.

Conclusion

A large number of women are suffering from the effects of growing up in a chemically dependent family and/or from being codependent. Growing awareness and acceptance of these problems has made it easier for women to identify themselves as adult children, codependents, or women who love too much. A large number of these women are prone to being chemically dependent themselves.

Treatment programs could attract a greater number of women clients if they were to provide services specifically designed for adult children, codependents, and women who love too much. Programs are debating which problems they should address first. It is imperative that people become abstinent and sober prior to dealing with other problems such as codependency and ACA issues. Nevertheless, it is also imperative that programs validate, respect, and work with each client's presenting problem.

The fact that so many counselors have been raised in chemically dependent families or families with similar systems might be extremely beneficial for their clients. It is not therapists' freedom from trauma, "but rather their ability to experience and articulate it that makes them sensitive to the problems of their patients. They can be more supportive in helping a patient experience his or her childhood traumas if they no longer need to fear the traumas of their own childhood or puberty" (Miller 1984, 185).

The work of healing can take place only within a treatment environment that understands the extent of these wounds and respects the arduous nature of the recovery process. Only then can the imprisoned child finally be set free to experience the full spectrum of her or his feelings and being. "The true opposite of depression is not gaiety or absence of pain, but vitality: the freedom to experience spontaneous feelings. It is part of the kaleidoscope of life that these feelings are not only cheerful, beautiful and good, they also can display the whole scale of human experience, including envy, jealousy, rage, disgust, greed, despair, and mourning" (Miller 1981, 57). Healing the narcissistic wounds of the adult so that she or he does not inflict these needs on another generation of children might prove to be prevention in its truest sense.

3

Chemical Dependency, Pregnancy, and Parenting

Assessment and Treatment Planning

Over the past five years, there has been a dramatic increase in the number of newborns diagnosed with intrauterine exposure to illicit drugs. This increase is represented in the following toxicology results from Martin Luther King Hospital in Los Angeles:

Year	Number of Positive Urines
1981	28 (Bean 1986)
1984	128 (Bean 1986)
1986	267 (Bean 1988)

Heightened awareness, more sophisticated urine screening techniques, and increased screening of groups at risk have all contributed to the increase in detected cases. In addition, it is believed that there has been an increase in the number of pregnant women who are using dangerous drugs during pregnancy.

Urine Screening

For urine screening to be effective, a number of precautions must be taken.

1. Collection of all urine specimens for toxicology should be

observed. Individuals collecting a urine specimen should be properly trained in observing the client. There are many ways to falsify a test, such as dipping the collecting bottle into the toilet water to dilute the specimen. If the specimen is improperly collected, negative results are meaningless.

2. Urine screening must be done randomly and on a surprise basis. If clients have time to prepare for a urine test, there are many ways they can falsify the test. Simply drinking large quantities of water prior to the test might dilute the sample sufficiently to produce a false negative result.

3. Specific toxicology tests must be requested. What is considered routine toxicology screening varies from lab to lab and frequently does not include testing for Valium, other prescription drugs, cocaine, or PCP (phencyclidine). A report of "no drugs detected" means that none of the drugs tested for were found, but such a report indicates nothing about drugs not included in that particular screen.

At Risk Groups

Routine urine screening should be performed by all hospitals on pregnant women who are obviously using or have used drugs. These include women who are on methadone, known drug users, women with tracks (scars from intravenous drug use), and women who have delivered other infants with drug withdrawal symptoms. A less obvious, but equally important, group are women who are at a high risk of having used drugs but do not present with a clear drug history. These include women who have received little or no prenatal care, women who deliver outside the obstetrical unit (for example, in the emergency room, the ambulance, or at home), and women who have precipitous deliveries. These last two situations are common in women who use drugs because they are not in touch with the process of labor and wait too long before entering the hospital. Testing both these women and their newborn infants may lead to the identification of a large but hidden at risk group and to the provision of more appropriate medical and social services.

Infants who are passively addicted should continue to be tested until they test negative. Documented negative tests prior to release from the hospital will demonstrate a therapeutic end point and will also be helpful if the infant returns with other drug ingestions. Hospital personnel must not discharge an infant prior to getting the results of the toxicology screen. If the newborn tests positive for a drug but has been discharged with the mother, it can be very difficult to find the mother and render the proper care to the infant. If the physician is concerned enough to order a toxicology screen, it is imperative that the infant be kept at the hospital until the results are received.

Specific Drugs

PCP

A dramatic increase in infants born with urine testing positive for PCP has been seen in some areas. The following figures from Martin Luther King Hospital in Los Angeles are illustrative of this trend:

Year	*Newborns Testing Positive for PCP*
1978–1980	28
1981	9
1982	30
1983	29
1984	97
1986	53 (Bean 1988)

The fetal effects of maternal PCP use include intrauterine growth retardation; delayed neonatal drug withdrawal, which might not be apparent until five to seven days postpartum; and developmental delays. Follow-up studies reveal significant long-term developmental disabilities. Infants symptomatic at birth might be displaying the acute drug effects—that is, intoxication. Withdrawal occurs later, since this drug is lipid soluble, is found in the fatty tissues, and tends to recirculate.

Cocaine

The incidence of infants born with urine testing positive for cocaine also has increased dramatically, as is indicated by the following statistics from the same Los Angeles hospital:

Year	Newborns Testing Positive for Cocaine
1981	1
1982	1
1983	2
1984	10
1985	93
1986	167 (Bean 1988)

This increase parallels the increased availability of inexpensive cocaine in the south-central areas of Los Angeles. It should be noted that routine screening for cocaine was not conducted at this hospital until 1985. Many hospitals still do not include cocaine in their routine toxicology screens.

Fetal effects of maternal cocaine use include prematurity, neonatal intoxication and withdrawal, cerebrovascular accidents, necrotizing enterocolitis (decreased blood supply to the gastrointestinal tract), decreased alertness as measured by the Brazelton Scale, and an increase in sudden infant death syndrome (SIDS) as follows:

1.6 per 1,000	General population
3 per 1,000	Methadone maintained mothers
8 per 1,000	Mothers using cocaine (Los Angeles statistics)
17 per 1,000	Mothers using cocaine (Chicago statistics)

At discharge, cocaine babies usually display symptoms that may include jitteriness, excessive crying, increased appetite, extreme irritability, and decreased consolability.

Alcohol

Depending on the study the fetal alcohol syndrome (FAS) has been reported in one out of every six hundred to one thousand births and is dose related. While full-blown FAS is believed to occur at 2 ounces of alcohol a day, significant neurological impairment in the infant can occur with the ingestion of only 1 ounce of alcohol a day by the pregnant woman. FAS includes brain injury, growth impairment, facial deformity, and congenital heart defects. The growth impairment is reflected in decreased length, weight, and head circumference. The microcephaly (small head) seen in many of these infants is associated with severe to moderate developmental disabilities, since the circumference of the head is a reflection of brain growth. The failure to thrive is not eradicated with increased feeding; these children are born small and remain small.

Fetal alcohol effects (FAE) are seen in the offspring of mothers who drink moderately. The effects include hyperactivity, low birth weight for gestational age, and some of the same symptoms that occur with FAS. FAS represents the tip of the iceberg, while FAE represents the large number of infants who are affected by the mother's alcohol use during pregnancy but whose disabilities might go undiagnosed and unappreciated.

Marijuana

Marijuana crosses the placenta and is found in breast milk. It is associated with small birth weight, decreased psychomotor performance, decreased ability to perform skilled tests, and decreased learning ability. The ingestion of marijuana together with alcohol potentiates the alcohol, and FAS is found five times more frequently in the offspring of mothers who use both alcohol and marijuana than in the offspring of mothers who use alcohol alone.

Cigarette Smoking

It is rare to find a woman addicted to alcohol and other drugs who does not smoke cigarettes. It has been known since 1957 that maternal cigarette smoking during pregnancy reduces the birth weight of the baby. Infants born to women who smoke weigh, on an average, 200 grams (7 ounces) less than babies born to nonsmoking women. The surgeon general has reported that 20 to 40 percent of low birth weight incidence in the United States is related to maternal smoking (DHHS 1980). Furthermore, the decrease in weight is directly correlated with the amount a woman smokes during pregnancy; that is, the more a woman smokes, the smaller her baby will be. This decrease in weight has been directly attributed to the deleterious effects of the carbon monoxide found in cigarette smoke.

Low birth weight is a reflection of intrauterine growth retardation and as such poses a significant risk to the newborn. Babies who are born full term but are small for their gestational age show increased mortality and morbidity and are at increased risk for cerebral palsy, malformations, and developmental disabilities. In addition, researchers have described a fetal tobacco syndrome, which includes adverse effects on the child's growth, intellectual development, and behavior. The fetal tobacco syndrome is attributed to the effects of nicotine and cyanide in cigarette smoke.

Maternal smoking also increases the risk of SIDS and has been clearly linked with obstetrical complications such as spontaneous abortion, fetal death, placenta previa (low implantation of the placenta), premature separation of the placenta, bleeding, and preterm delivery.

Diazepam (Valium) and Other Benzodiazepines

Diazepam accumulates in fetal tissues in high concentrations. Even after low and moderate chronic treatment (10 to 15 milligrams per day) in a pregnant woman, the pharmacological actions of the drug might be sustained in her baby for eight to ten days after birth. Typically, symptoms at birth are secondary to acute intoxication. That is, at birth the infant is experiencing the inebriating effects of the drug; once the drug is eliminated from the infant's body, withdrawal will occur. There is a delayed onset of withdrawal symptoms with longer acting drugs such as diazepam. Fetal effects of chronic low-dose or acute high-dose maternal diazepam use include lethargy, respiratory difficulties, apneic spells, disturbances in thermoregulation, hypotonia, and failure to suck effectively.

Barbiturates

The effects of barbiturates on the newborn have been studied in conjunction with mothers who take these drugs for treatment of seizure disorders. A syndrome very similar to FAS has been described for offspring of women who take barbiturates and dilantin.

Again, the baby might first appear to be acutely intoxicated with the barbiturate, but as the barbiturate is cleared from the body, the infant will move from a state of intoxication to withdrawal. This is dependent on the chronicity of use, the amount used, the last dose, and whether the mother was taking shorter or longer acting barbiturates. Symptoms of barbiturate withdrawal might not occur until four to seven days after birth. These symptoms include tremulousness, restlessness, a persistent high-pitched cry, sleeplessness, and hyperreflexia. They can lead to convulsions if not properly managed.

Despite this, women who must take barbiturates for seizure control are not urged to detoxify prior to birth, as seizures themselves can be very dangerous to both maternal and fetal health. It should be noted that the dose women take for control of seizures is typically much lower than the dose used by individuals who are psychologically dependent.

Narcotics

This category includes both heroin and methadone. While narcotic withdrawal in adults is typically not life threatening, narcotic withdrawal in infants can be.

Heroin and methadone are both narcotics but have properties that affect the pregnant woman and the fetus differently. Heroin is an appetite suppressant, and pregnant women on heroin often have babies who are small for gestational age. Methadone does not have this anorectic effect, and babies born of mothers who conceived on moderate doses of methadone or who were maintained on methadone soon after conception tend to be larger than those of heroin using mothers.

Heroin is a shorter acting drug than methadone, and this difference affects the onset, duration, and intensity of withdrawal. Heroin addicted babies will begin to experience withdrawal within four to twenty-four hours after delivery. Methadone dependent babies may show symptoms of withdrawal anywhere from the end of the first day to two weeks postpartum; the average time for onset of methadone withdrawal is seventy-two hours after delivery. Many infants born to mothers who are maintained at 20 milligrams of methadone or less and who are not using other drugs may not demonstrate visible signs of narcotic withdrawal. Methadone withdrawal tends to be less intense than heroin withdrawal but might last longer. In addition, while heroin withdrawal typically escalates and then abates in a stepwise fashion, methadone withdrawal can be biphasic, appearing subdued at times and then becoming more intense.

Neonatal narcotic abstinence syndrome includes the following characteristics: central nervous system (CNS) hyperirritability; gastrointestinal dysfunction, including regurgitation and diarrhea; respiratory distress; and vague autonomic symptoms of yawning, mottling, sneezing, and fever. The hallmarks of the CNS irritability are tremors, hypertonicity, hyperreflexia, restlessness, insomnia, increased sucking reflex but difficulty in coordinating sucking and swallowing, and a high-pitched cry.

Infants who are prenatally exposed to multiple drugs do worse than infants who are exposed to methadone alone. Pregnant women on methadone should be monitored very carefully. The presence of prenatal care is a positive prognosticator for fetal and neonatal outcome; the more prenatal care a woman receives, the better the expected outcome.

The following guidelines will help enhance the outcome of the pregnancy:

1. Prenatal care should be made a mandatory part of the methadone program for pregnant women.

2. Methadone levels should not be higher than 40 milligrams per day.

3. Urine should be tested three times a week.

4. Women whose urine tests positive for other drugs should be confronted with their positive test results immediately, and a plan for corrective action should be designed.

5. Women who continue to use heroin or other drugs in conjunction with the methadone should be tapered off metha-

done. Pregnant addicts must understand the deleterious effects of mixing these drugs, and the program should be clear that it will not participate in dually addicting the fetus.

Detoxification. Fetal withdrawal in utero carries a high risk of morbidity and mortality. To prevent fetal withdrawal, either careful and slow detoxification with an agonist or maintenance therapy can be used. It is safest to detoxify the mother between the fourteenth and twenty-eighth week of pregnancy, but it is important to remember that detoxification might be a naive and unrealistic goal (NIDA 1979). For women who were unable to detoxify prior to pregnancy, the discomforts of pregnancy might make detoxification even more difficult. Many women who attempt detoxification during this time end up using heroin and other drugs. It is probably more realistic to put a woman on a low-dose methadone program and offer social and therapeutic support during this difficult period.

If detoxification is attempted, the woman should be put on 20 milligrams of methadone and then reduced 5 milligrams every other week. For maintenance, a dose of 30 milligrams a day is a good level, providing that the woman is not using other drugs (NIDA 1979). If the woman can be slowly detoxified to 20 milligrams or less, it certainly makes the management of the neonate much easier, but this should be attempted only if the woman is clean from other drugs, stabilized, and cooperative.

Breast Feeding. It is advisable to permit breast feeding for a mother who is well controlled on a stable dose of methadone, in a well-supervised treatment program, motivated to nurse her infant, and not using other drugs. Breast feeding for longer than six months is probably inadvisable because of the increased quantities of breast milk and, hence, drug the older infant would ingest (NIDA 1979).

Reporting Requirements

There are no uniform reporting regulations governing hospitals once an infant is determined to be passively addicted. In some areas, state or local regulations make it mandatory for the hospital to report all cases of neonatal withdrawal. These regulations are based on the premise that the use of dangerous drugs during pregnancy constitutes child abuse and deserves further investigation. Some hospitals have established their own policies demanding that these cases be reported to child protective services, even in the absence of state or local regulations.

In general, there is a move toward more rigorous reporting and evaluation of pregnant drug dependent women largely because of the more compelling information now available about the enduring effects of growing up in dysfunctional, drug dependent families. In the 1960s and early 1970s, there was a push for family reunification. This is still an excellent goal, but time and experience have led us to understand the deep challenge these very wounded women present. Many child protective agencies have come to understand that traditional treatment plans are often unable to rehabilitate the mother sufficiently to provide adequate care for her child and protect the child from either the mother's own violence or violence perpetrated by her partner.

It is imperative that drug programs know the local regulations and hospital policies governing the reporting of addicted newborns. Networking among drug programs, hospitals, and child protective agencies is essential to ensure proper identification, assessment, and treatment planning for these women and their children.

The following guidelines will help a community to identify the chemically dependent pregnant woman and the passively addicted newborn:

1. Every community and hospital should develop policies regarding the reporting of newborns found to be passively addicted to dangerous drugs.

2. Child protective services should be notified of every infant who is found to be passively addicted to dangerous drugs.

3. Hospitals should initiate drug screenings for mothers who are known or suspected of using drugs and participating in other high-risk behaviors. Pregnant women who received little or no prenatal care, women who delivered in areas

other than the delivery room, and women who experienced a precipitous delivery should all be screened.

4. Methadone programs should develop ways of working closely with child protective services. One county in California makes all female and male methadone clients sign a note of understanding that the program will report any suspected case of child neglect and abuse. While federally funded methadone programs are obligated to abide by the client confidentiality rules, they are also (through different regulations) obligated to report cases of suspected child abuse and neglect.

Assessment of the
Chemically Dependent Woman's Risk
for Abusing Her Child

While all women who continue to use illicit drugs during pregnancy are at risk for abusing or neglecting their children, some women are at greater risk than others. Assessment of relative risk must serve as the cornerstone of placement decisions and treatment planning. While drug programs are often asked to make judgments in this area, they frequently lack the necessary background and expertise in child development and parenting assessment to do so properly. Alternatively, social service workers are often at a disadvantage in this situation because they do not know how to assess the chemical dependency side of the problem. In addition, they might not be aware of the drug and alcohol services available in the community and might lack experience in matching the client to the right treatment modality.

The Woman's History

Taking the following history is essential in evaluation whether a mother is at a high, low, or moderate risk for abusing and neglecting her children.

Physical and/or Sexual Abuse of the Mother as a Child. If the mother has experienced physical and sexual abuse as a child and if she has not received effective treatment, she is at risk for believing that this is an acceptable child-rearing practice. In addition, victims of this type of abuse have deep wounds and might lack the boundary differentiation necessary to see their children's needs as different from their own (see chapter 2).

Family Violence. Violence in the mother's family of origin, even if not directed at her, might be indicative of a dysfunctional family style that the mother is prone to repeat unless she receives effective treatment.

Mother's Own Childhood Placement in Foster Care. If the mother was placed in foster care as a child, this might indicate a level of disorganization in the family of origin. Since some women find it difficult to discuss violence and abuse in their family of origin, having this information can indirectly lead the interviewer to a greater understanding of the family environment.

Chemical Dependency in Family of Origin. Alcoholism and other drug dependencies are often found in the families of chemically dependent women. The biochemical, genetic, and environmental factors involved in this pattern all influence the mother's coping style. This information is also important when evaluating other family members for potential placement of the infant. The courts and child protective agencies should be particularly careful of the almost automatic response of placing the infant with the maternal grandmother. The involvement of the maternal grandmother in her daughter's life is often a sign of enmeshment and is not indicative of a positive support network. Loni's situation, described in case 1 of the chapter appendix, is a good example. The judge suggested that the maternal grandmother take custody of the child, but an anonymous call to child protective services revealed that the grandmother was an alcoholic who had physically abused her own children. A thorough evaluation confirmed that the grandmother would not be an appropriate guardian. In general there should be greater appreciation of the reality that, more often than not, chemically dependent women come from severely dysfunctional families.

Prior Attempts at Drug Treatment. Successful attempts at prior treatment might be encouraging indicators of the woman's ability to engage in a therapeutic alliance. Alternatively, a history of multiple treatment failures and resistance to entering treatment might indicate that the woman will not be able to be successful in such a program. Such a history often represents the presence of strong denial on the part of the woman. Even in the face of serious adverse consequences, both to themselves and their newborns, many women will insist that they really do not have a problem and do not need help.

In evaluating prior treatment attempts, it is imperative to ask how long the client stayed in treatment and whether she successfully completed the program. For example, in case 2 of the chapter appendix, Grace reported that she had been in a residential program (therapeutic community). On further questioning it was revealed that she had left after only six hours.

Other Children. Asking questions about the birth weight of other children can help determine whether these children were exposed to drugs during the prenatal period. It is also important to ask specific questions regarding the location of other children. Often these women will list all their children, give their names, ages, and birth weights, and even discuss how they are doing in school but fail to mention that some of these children do not live with them. Sometimes the children have been removed because of neglect and abuse; in other situations, no formal custody hearing was held, but other family members removed the children because of concern about the woman's ability to care for them.

It is, therefore, imperative to garner information concerning the well-being and functioning of other children directly from schools and physicians. Grace reported that all her other children were doing well and were A students. When the caseworker contacted the school, she heard a very different story. One child had a severe learning disability and a hearing deficit that the mother had failed to have evaluated even after repeated requests by the school. Another child was doing very poorly and had to repeat the first grade. The school also reported that the mother had been hostile and uncooperative. In contacting the pediatrician of another client, it was found that he had been concerned about the mother's treatment of her two children and felt that if the children were left with the mother, they would wind up dead.

Isolation. Families that are isolated from the mainstream of society are at increased risk for abusing and neglecting their children. Both physical and social isolation must be considered. A woman with few supports and with friends who are also drug dependent will face added stress in trying to stay off drugs and in raising her children. Grace, for example, lived miles away from the nearest bus route and did not have a current driver's license; in this case, part of the plan for family reunification was for her to obtain a driver's license.

Socioeconomic Status. While both chemical dependency and child abuse and neglect cut across all segments of society, poverty exacerbates these problems. It is important to consider how the mother will support herself if she is no longer involved with illegal drug activities.

History of Spouse or Partner. Chemically dependent women often have chemically dependent partners. Frequently, it is not the woman herself but her partner who physically abuses her children. In these situations, the woman cannot protect either herself or her children from the physical violence. In fact, many of these women may actively seek out abusive, sadistic men to balance their own masochistic tendencies.

A case in point is a young woman I evaluated for Child Protective Services who left home at age sixteen to live with an older heroin dependent man who beat her. She left him, only to find other men who would beat her and her children. The last man she was with had actually been jailed in another county for beating a former wife. His violence escalated to the point where he kept the woman prisoner for twenty-four hours and brutally beat one of her children. Even after this violent rampage, the woman said she still wanted to be with him; the woman also said that she found men who were nice to her boring. As a child, she had been beaten by her mother, removed from the home for this abuse, then placed back in her mother's home years later, only to be beaten again. Violence was the only way this woman knew to relate to other people.

The opposite of this is also true. The presence of a partner who is drug-free and does not have a history of antisocial behavior can be a critical supportive element in the reunification plan.

Other Factors

In addition to using a thorough history to assess the mother's strengths and weaknesses, referring to the flowchart in figure 3–1 might help separate out women who fall into higher risk groups for child abuse and neglect from those who have a lower risk.

Clearly, women who enter treatment during the pregnancy and stay clean are displaying a higher level of functioning than those who fail to do so; they are able to put their babies' needs ahead of their own. Some women are unable to experience the reality of their babies until they are born. These women may continue to use drugs during pregnancy, but upon seeing their infants, they are able to enter treatment and begin to get their lives together. The highest risk group is composed of women who never clean up during their pregnancy and continue to deny the effects of their drug taking behavior even when they see their babies go through withdrawal. These women often blame the doctors and nurses for their infants' discomfort. One woman, for example, said the doctor gave her baby a drug in the nursery that made the baby jittery.

Again, a case history might be instructive. Samantha (case 3 in the chapter appendix) failed to get prenatal care during her pregnancy although she had received such care during a prior pregnancy. She continued to use heroin, cocaine, and alcohol during the entire pregnancy and was at a bar when labor started. The baby was born prematurely, suffering from both gonorrhea and neonatal narcotic abstinence syndrome. The infant was placed in a foster home, and the mother was told that she would have to enter drug treatment in order to get her child back. Although Samantha

Figure 3–1. *Assessing Risk for Child Abuse and Neglect by the Chemically Dependent Woman*

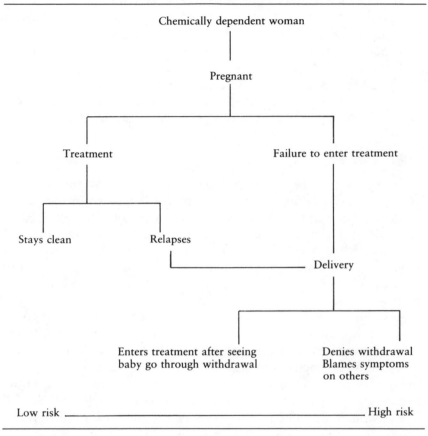

said she wanted her child back, she did nothing to demonstrate that this desire was sincere.

Samantha missed three appointments for evaluation of her chemical dependency and risk for abusing her child. When she kept a fourth appointment, she showed up obviously drunk. Urine tests during this period were positive for cocaine. Her older sister also used heroin and lost custody of her children because of her drug use. Samantha's failure to abstain from drugs and to keep appointments even when her child had been removed and she knew she was being evaluated did not bode well for her future behavior.

Three months after Samantha was ordered by the court into residential drug treatment, she still had not made any attempt to enter such a program. In addition, she continually missed appointments to see her baby.

Initially, she had acted as if she was not pregnant and, once she delivered, she acted as if she did not have a child. When the baby was removed, Samantha verbally insisted that she wanted her child back, but she was unwilling or unable to take any steps that would have brought this about. In fact, she repeatedly sabotaged plans that could have led to reunification. Basically, she did not act like a woman who wanted her child.

It is imperative that such women ultimately be evaluated by what they do and not by what they say. It takes a high level of functioning for a woman to appropriately assess her ability to care for a child. Most of these women do not have that ability. While they may not want their children, they are not functioning at a level that would permit them to give the children up for adoption.

Developing a Treatment Plan for the Chemically Dependent Mother

The treatment plan must be based on a detailed assessment of the mother's strengths and needs. The more at risk a woman is, the more structured her plan and treatment must be. Multiple behavioral changes and goals must be used as milestones against which each woman's growth can be measured.

Abstinence from drugs is only one measurement of the woman's ability to care for her child. Sobriety and abstinence, while essential for rehabilitation, are not sufficient to ensure that the woman will now be able to care for her children adequately. For the majority of these women, chemical dependency is only one part of their problem.

The courts are often insensitive to these complexities and rely on negative urine tests as the sole indication of the mother's level of functioning. There are many chemically dependent women who know enough to stop using drugs during pregnancy, do not have violent spouses, and would not let themselves be battered. To measure a woman's functioning accurately, multiple parameters must be used, including keeping appointments, quality of visitations with the child, engagement in drug treatment, participation in parenting classes, attention to her own medical needs, vocational training, legal obligations, education, financial management, establishing a supportive non–drug using network, recreational activities, and linkages to self-help groups such as Alcoholics Anonymous, Narcotics Anonymous, and AL-ANON.

Many of these women are functioning at a low level and may be experiencing some transient neurological deficits due to their drug and alcohol use. These deficits should be kept in mind when establishing a treatment plan. A good rule is to keep the plan simple and not to attempt to do everything at once. This will only overwhelm the woman and sabotage the reunification. Plans that phase in increased responsibility and move from greater structure to less structure will be more manageable. The treatment goals should be broken down into bite-size pieces so that the women can experience success early in the recovery process.

Women who present a moderate to high risk should be considered for residential treatment, which offers an excellent environment for learning social skills and increased responsibility. Outpatient programming is often not structured or intense enough to afford these women the support they need. While a few residential programs are currently prepared to take pregnant women and women with children into treatment, all communities should have such programs available to them.

Conclusion

Use of drugs during pregnancy has severe adverse consequences for the fetus and newborn. With many drugs, these consequences are prolonged and can lead to enduring deficits in the child. Vigorous systems should be in place to identify chemically dependent pregnant women and to provide appropriate treatment for these mothers and their children.

Drug use is often just one of many problems these women have. Chemically dependent women, especially heroin dependent women, are often products of child abuse and neglect. Strict sex role socialization, emotional neglect as infants, and criticism and punishment for failing to live up to their parents' premature demands typify the pattern under which these women were raised. Society and family foster traits of alienation, dependency, low self-esteem, and a severely diminished capacity to enjoy life. A neglected and abused child grows up to become a needy and dependent adult. Without adequate intervention, these women will repeat the same family patterns with their own children (Mondanaro 1977).

When social service agencies are asked to evaluate the drug dependent mother and her passively addicted newborn, they should understand that they have two clients who are in need of protection and treatment: the mother and her child. Aggressive treatment planning and networking among the court system, child protective agencies, parenting programs, and drug treatment programs is essential to intervene effectively in this deeply rooted generational cycle.

Appendix 3A: Case Examples

Case 1

January 20, 1986
To: Child Protective Services
From: Josette Mondanaro, M.D.

I am writing regarding my evaluation of Loni and her mother, Betty, as requested by Child Protective Services. I interviewed both Loni and Betty on January 7, 1986, and January 15, 1986.

Background

Loni is a twenty-three-year-old woman who delivered a 5 pound ¼ ounce full-term baby girl on November 14, 1985. The appearance of intrauterine growth retardation and the development of jitteriness in the infant cued the attending pediatrician into the fact that the infant was experiencing the effects of passive prenatal exposure to drugs.

Loni gave a history of using cocaine and alcohol and of smoking cigarettes during the pregnancy. The pediatrician noted that Loni had an unusual and volatile affect just a few hours after delivery. Loni's urine drug screen was positive for THC (marijuana) and cocaine.

The case was referred to Child Protective Services and the infant placed in a foster home. It is my understanding that at the first hearing the judge requested that consideration be given to placing the infant with Loni's mother, Betty. Following that, Child

Protective Services received an anonymous call which said that Betty was an alcoholic who had been abusive to her own children, including Loni. The following is my evaluation of Betty and Loni.

Family History

Betty is a sixty-five-year-old woman who has been married to Hal, age seventy-six, for thirty-three years. Prior to her marriage to Hal, Betty was married to Cam. She has two natural children and one adopted daughter.

Betty ran a foster home and says that approximately twenty-six children were placed in her home. From this foster home, Betty adopted three more children when her first set of children were becoming adults and leaving home. She adopted two boys and Loni all at about the same time. Loni's biological mother gave her up at birth, and Betty took Loni from the hospital.

Loni's Past History

Loni gives a history of a troubled youth. She repeatedly ran away from home when she was eleven to twelve years old and received family counseling at Youth Services. She reports that she left home when she was sixteen years old and became an emancipated minor. She went to school and worked part-time. In 1980, Loni received her GED through adult education.

When she was twenty-one years old, Loni moved back home. Loni says that her mother moved out of the home six years ago to cope with her uterine cancer. Loni lived with her father and her two brothers. Loni then moved out again in March 1985.

Loni states that this is her fourth pregnancy. She first became pregnant at eighteen years of age and has had two miscarriages and one ectopic pregnancy. She says that she has never used birth control and has been trying to get pregnant in order to have someone to love her.

Drug History

Loni states that she has used marijuana, cocaine, alcohol, and "whites" (speed) and smokes cigarettes. She reveals herself to be more experienced with drugs than she admits. For example, she stated that when she first snorted cocaine she didn't think it was any big deal because it just felt like the "whites" she took from 1979 to 1980 when she worked the graveyard shift at a convalescent hospital. She said that other workers introduced her to the "whites" and this was the way they made it through the night.

During the second interview, Loni denied taking "whites." She also denied liking cocaine and said it made her sick.

Loni says that during the first three months of pregnancy, she decreased her cigarette smoking to six cigarettes a day because she knew the cigarette smoking would be harmful to the baby. I asked her "What would make a smart woman like you, who knew cigarette smoking would be harmful to her baby, use cocaine?" Loni basically blames other people for her drug use and fails to see her responsibility.

Her denial is so entrenched that she cannot see that her drug use during pregnancy affected the size of her baby. She believes that her baby was small and jittery because she had root canal work, a cold, and a cyst removed during pregnancy.

Loni says that she lives at home because she doesn't want her seventy-six-year-old father to live alone. She is afraid that he will die soon, although her mother denies that he is ill except for lower back pain.

Relationships with Men

Ricky, the baby's father, has been in and out of jail because of drunk driving arrests, driving with a suspended license, and violating parole. From April to July 4, 1985, Loni was dating Billy. He, too, is an alcoholic, and they had violent fights. She denies that he hit her but admits to hitting him. On July 4 she broke up with Billy and tried to get Ricky back. She felt she needed him to be able to emotionally and financially meet the burden of parenting. On July 26, 1985, Ricky was released from jail and rejected Loni. She says she felt so devastated by his rejection that she started using cocaine.

Loni stated that when she was eight months pregnant, Ricky was driving drunk and tried to run her off the road following a fight. She said she called the police, and he was arrested for driving with a suspended license. She says he was released from jail recently but may be going to prison for three more years. She says she needs him and will continue to try to get him back.

Tim is Loni's twenty-three-year-old adopted brother. One year ago he was drunk and punched Loni. She states that her nose was broken in two places and she was hospitalized. Their relationship has always been volatile, and following this altercation Loni put a restraining order on Tim.

Relationship to the Infant

Loni repeatedly says that she prayed to God to give her a baby in order to give meaning to her life. She feels like her life will be better with a baby. She stated that she has needed someone to love her and a baby would be that person.

Her mother, Betty, was forced to comment on this role reversal. She told Loni that the baby needed her and that it couldn't just be Loni needing the baby. The family physician also recognized this unhealthy role reversal; in her report dated December 17, 1985, she states, "Loni has the unrealistic view that all she needs to make her happy is to get her baby back."

Evaluation of the Grandmother (Betty)

Betty is a sixty-five-year-old woman who has multiple medical problems including hypertension, osteoarthritis, and rheumatoid arthritis. She continues to live alone since she moved out of the family's house in 1981. She said she moved out when she was diagnosed as having uterine cancer. The cancer has been cured, and she continues to live alone to avoid all the disruptions which occur when she lives with her family.

She does not want custody of the infant and believes that the court would not give her the child because of her age and medical ailments. She says she would like to see Loni get a chance at trying to raise the baby and she would help. She then states that, considering all the problems with pot, alcohol, and cocaine, perhaps she didn't do such a good job with her own kids, but blames their friends for all their problems.

Betty adamantly denies drinking or having an alcohol problem. She states that her last drink was in June when she had a vodka and orange juice. Her physical appearance and indeed, more importantly, her blood tests argue against her assertion.

Betty's blood panel taken on 1/7/86 were consistent with alcoholism and the acute ingestion of large quantities of alcohol. Grossly elevated liver enzyme GGTP in the face of normal values for the other liver enzymes, decreased red blood cell count, and increased red blood cell size are all consistent with the diagnosis of alcoholism.

The GGTP will begin to fall back to a normal range within four weeks of not drinking. When Betty was presented with this information, she said that she had taken Nyquil the night before the test. I explained that Nyquil, in its usual prescribed dose, would not have changed this liver enzyme and her red blood cells. I offered to have the test repeated if Betty felt there was an error, and she refused.

On each occasion I interviewed Betty and Loni separately and then together, Betty's harsh and critical manner of dealing with Loni was particularly distressing. While Betty was present to offer support, treating Loni like an immature, irresponsible, unknowledgeable preteen did not add to the picture of Loni as a competent, capable young woman.

Summary

Clearly, Loni wants her child back, but there are a number of points in this case which do not bode well for a positive outcome. Her mother's alcoholism is adamantly denied in the face of strong medical evidence. The family fails to grasp or even consider the interconnectedness of the son's alcoholism and violence, Loni's chemical dependency, Betty's alcoholism, and the fact that Loni continues to select boyfriends who are alcoholic and violent. In addition, the family insists that if there were any problems they were in the past and were caused by the bad influence of others.

Loni's wish for a child to love her and her sense that the baby will take care of her needs, fill her emptiness, and make her life worthwhile is a serious role reversal which reflects her own troubled life. Unable to find the parenting she needs in her parents, unable to find the romantic love she desires in Ricky and other men, she has turned to having a baby in the hope that finally she will be loved and cared for.

Betty appears to be too physically ill to be able to assist Loni with the responsibilities of parenting. Ricky, the baby's father, is a violent alcoholic whose presence should be a cause for concern. Loni admits that all her friends use drugs and alcohol. The strengths and supports in this system are not apparent and, indeed, may not exist.

After careful consideration, I believe that there are two people in this case who are in need of assistance and protection: the infant and Loni herself. The infant cannot be helped until Loni is helped.

It is my recommendation that Loni enter a long-term residential drug rehabilitation program in order to treat her chemical dependency and to assist her in developing the maturity she now lacks. In addition, such a rehabilitation program would help her develop a more positive support system, enhance her self-esteem, and break her dependence on violent alcoholic men.

I strongly urge you not to consider outpatient treatment for Loni. I believe that outpatient treatment will not provide Loni with the formal structure and support she needs. Also, until and unless Loni develops the above-mentioned skills and successfully completes a drug treatment program, I believe that the well-being of the infant will be seriously compromised.

Please call me should you have further questions regarding this case.

Case 2

To: Child Protective Services
From: Josette Mondanaro, M.D.

I am writing regarding Grace. I interviewed Grace at your office on February 7 and 17, 1986.

Background

Grace is a thirty-four-year-old woman who gave birth to a 6 pound 3 ounce girl on January 25, 1986. According to the mother, the baby was one month premature. The mother states she was using heroin intravenously for the last trimester of pregnancy. The infant was noted to develop irritability and jitteriness on the second day of life consistent with neonatal narcotic withdrawal. The infant was placed in a foster home pending the outcome of an evaluation of this case.

Drug History

Grace states that she started using heroin when she was twenty-one to twenty-two years old. She has used heroin intermittently since that time. The presence of large needle scars (tracks) on her hands, forearms, and anticubital fossae attest to the chronicity and longevity of her use of heroin.

Grace denies using other drugs prior to heroin. She states that she tried pot once and it made her paranoid. She denies any history of glue or paint sniffing or PCP use. She does admit to using diet pills when she was trying to lose weight in 1970 to 1971. She says she drinks beer twice a month and has cut down her cigarette smoking to one to two cigarettes a day.

Besides being treated for neonatal narcotic withdrawal, the infant was also treated for hepatitis A and B. Grace said that she became a carrier of hepatitis secondary to using IV heroin.

She has had legal problems secondary to her use and sale of drugs. Grace says she sold heroin to support her heroin habit. She was arrested for driving under the influence and admits to being loaded on heroin at the time. She was also arrested for driving without a license. In 1981, Grace went to state prison for twenty-eight months for possession and sale of narcotics.

Prior to entering prison she was told that her case would go better if she entered a drug treatment facility. Grace entered a residential program and did not complete a full day there before leaving.

Although she admits to a seventeen-year history of narcotic

dependency, Grace does not believe she has a drug problem. In addition, she does not believe she needs chemical dependency treatment. Grace said that all she needed to stop using were her kids. I commented that she had her children for seventeen years and that had not stopped her from using.

Grace says that she knew the heroin would hurt the baby. She had a friend who was using heroin and went to her house to help her stay clean, but ended up using heroin herself.

Family of Origin

Grace was sixth in a family of ten children. She dropped out of high school in the second year. She worked in canneries and moved out of her mother's house when she was sixteen years old. She reports that her father has always had a drinking problem.

Relationship History

Grace met Joe and became pregnant at seventeen years old. She has related to Joe for the past seventeen years, and he has fathered four of her six children, including this new baby.

Joe usually lives with his parents but is presently in jail. He was in jail three times last year. Grace stated that she did not know why Joe was in jail, adding that he doesn't discuss anything with her. She does admit that he uses heroin. After the interview, the caseworker told me that Joe was in jail on drug charges.

Children

Grace has six children as follows: Joey, sixteen years; Richard, eleven years; Justine, seven years; David, six years; Sam, four years; Mary, three weeks. Grace says that all her children were large at birth and weighed between 9 and 10 pounds.

In 1981, when Grace went to prison, the children were cared for by relatives. Joey decided to remain with his paternal grandparents since that time. She did not see her children for twenty-eight months while in prison. Sam lives with his paternal aunt, and Grace says that she sees him every three to four months.

During the second interview, when confronted with information regarding David, Grace admitted that he was premature at seven months and weighed 3 pounds at birth. David has had ear and hearing difficulties which were diagnosed while Grace was in prison. She states that he is also "hyper" and acts out a lot. Sometimes he is quite shy. The schools are requesting further evaluation of David's hearing difficulties, and there is belief that this is affecting his speech. Grace was unaware of these problems.

According to school officials, Justine is repeating the first grade. This information regarding Justine and David is substantially different from the information given to me by Grace in the first interview.

When questioned as to what effect she felt her heroin use had on her children, she answered "none." She states that Joey knows that both she and Joe use heroin, but feels secure that this will not affect him because he says he doesn't want to use drugs.

Grace says that her children do very well in school and get A's and B's. Following that discussion the caseworker informed me that the schools called Grace regarding her children and found her to be uncooperative. Grace told me that she refused to permit the caseworker to talk to the schools.

Conclusion

Grace is in a strong state of denial regarding the effects of her heroin use. While she is pleasant, she remains uncooperative about the details of this case. She is saying what she thinks will make a good impression without understanding how bizarre her story sounds. For example, she states that she has been using heroin, off and on, for seventeen years but doesn't have a drug problem. She says that if she had a drug problem, she would tell me. She states that she knew the heroin would hurt her unborn baby, but she couldn't stop using. She says she doesn't have a drug problem and that the drug use during pregnancy "just happened."

It is not unusual for a chemically dependent person to be in denial about her drug problem. What troubles me about this case is the degree of Grace's denial in the face of such overwhelming evidence as neonatal withdrawal, her large tracks, and her own admissions.

During the second interview, I explained the disease of chemical dependency, including denial, the genetic biochemical influences, and the fact that this was a chronic progressive relapsing disease. Grace did become more cooperative when I explained that she is not responsible for having the disease of chemical dependency but is responsible for her recovery.

Grace's social isolation adds to the risk factors in this case. She states that she lives far away from bus lines, does not have a telephone, and does not possess a driver's license. She says that all she has to do is renew her license and she will have access to cars. From what I observed on Monday, it appears that she does drive without a license.

Grace's chronic heroin use, level of denial, social isolation, use of heroin during pregnancy, and failure to effectively note and follow through on David's hearing and possible speech problems all make this a high-risk situation. The continued presence of Joe, who is also a heroin addict, adds to the stress in this family.

While I would wish to see Grace reunited with her daughter, I believe that this can only come about through a vigorously monitored treatment plan. Grace wants what is best for her children, but she needs much help and support.

To reunite this family and to prevent further abuse and neglect, I am proposing a two-stage plan. In stage 1 Grace should do the following:

1. Enter either Alto or the Drug Treatment Program at Women's Crisis Support.

2. Undergo random urine toxicology screens, with the urine collection being observed by someone who is trained in this process.

3. Get a driver's license.

4. Have David's hearing and speech problems evaluated by a specialist and have a treatment plan designed.

5. Attend three Narcotics Anonymous (NA) or Alcoholics Anonymous (AA) meetings weekly.

6. Attend three AL-ANON meetings weekly.

7. Work the twelve-step programs in NA and AL-ANON and get sponsors in both programs.

8. Have attendance at all these meetings verified in writing.

9. Increase visitations with Mary.

In addition, during stage 1 all the other children, including Joey, should be thoroughly evaluated by Child Protective Services (CPS).

After these initial steps are taken, the case can be reviewed, and pending successful completion of the above, then Grace could be reunited with Mary. Stage 2 would include:

1. Monitoring and case management by CPS

2. Weekly counseling at a drug treatment program

3. Attendance and participation in AA, NA, and AL-ANON.

Hopefully, Grace will work cooperatively with CPS for her own recovery and the well-being of her family. Please contact me should you have any further questions.

Case 3

To: Child Protective Services
From: Josette Mondanaro, M.D.

I am writing regarding Samantha who was sent to me for evaluation of her chemical dependency.

Samantha failed to show for three separate scheduled appointments on 3/21/85, 4/1/85, and 4/10/85. After her failure to show on 4/10/85, I spoke with you and you told me that you saw Samantha earlier that day. You said that the patient did plan to keep the appointment and turned down a ride you offered, saying she had another ride to my office. I did see Samantha on 3/27/85 and obtained a detailed history from her at that time.

It is my understanding that on 3/15/85 Samantha gave birth to a 4 pound baby. Samantha was noted as having multiple track marks, and the baby did have neonatal narcotic withdrawal a few days later. It is also my understanding that Samantha was at a bar when her waters broke. The baby was born three weeks prematurely and had gonorrhea.

Samantha says she started using heroin one and a half to two years ago. When she became pregnant, she said she did not get prenatal care. She said she "thought about getting prenatal care a lot" but didn't do it because she said she was "thinking about drugs too much."

When I questioned her regarding frequency of heroin use, she said she used twice a month. When I told her that babies don't become addicted at this frequency, she then said she used twice weekly. Samantha admitted to using heroin since her baby was born and said she had used last week.

Samantha gives a history of sniffing paint. She says she was put in juvenile hall when she was seventeen years old. She continued to sniff paint until she became pregnant with her three-and-a-half-year-old.

Samantha reports that her older sister also uses heroin and lives at home with Samantha and her mother. Supposedly the mother had reported her sister to Child Protective Services because she was using drugs and neglecting her children.

Samantha showed up on 3/27/85 appearing intoxicated, with slurred speech and unsteady gait. Exam revealed multiple old and fresh tracks bilateral in the antecubital fossae. Patient's hands, nails, and arms were filthy.

From the thickened tracks, it was quite clear that Samantha's heroin use was more frequent and chronic than she had stated. Clearly she had minimized her drug use in her history. A urine toxicology screen was positive for cocaine on 3/27/85.

Samantha falls into an extremely high risk group for abusing and neglecting her child. She failed to get any prenatal care during the entire pregnancy and continued to use heroin, cocaine, and alcohol during the pregnancy. Perhaps most telling is her inability or unwillingness to stop drug use and keep appointments after the baby was removed from her.

Samantha's failure to abstain from drug use and to keep appointments even after her child had been removed and when she knew she was being evaluated does not bode well for her future behavior. This inability or unwillingness to take appropriate steps to present herself in a positive light reflects the level of her dysfunctioning and is a negative prognosticator.

It is my understanding that while Samantha was court ordered into a residential program in April, as of today (July 29, 1985) she has not made any attempt to enter such a program.

From my telephone conversation with you today, it is my understanding that Samantha continues to use heroin, is frequently loaded, and misses appointments to see her infant in foster care.

Basically Samantha acts as though this infant was never born. She did get prenatal care for her first child, who was full term and weighed a healthy eight pounds at birth. But she failed to get prenatal care for the second pregnancy and acted as if she weren't pregnant.

I would urge permanency planning for the infant in view of the mother's extreme behavior. Through her actions she has repeatedly sabotaged plans that could have led to reunification. Samantha acts as if she does not want her child.

The infant received no prenatal care, was born three weeks prematurely, and suffered from gonorrhea and neonatal narcotic addiction. Samantha consistently and continuously chooses drugs over her son's well-being and has done nothing to demonstrate any interest in reunification with this child.

In light of the above, I believe that the infant's best interests would be served by being adopted into a healthy family that would bond to him. I would not recommend placement with the grandmother or the immediate family because of the history of heroin use.

Please feel free to call me about this case if you should have any other questions.

Case 4

January 22, 1986
To: Child Protective Services
From: Josette Mondanaro, M.D.
Re: Ann

Ann is a twenty-five-year-old woman who delivered a 6 pound 10¾ ounce girl on January 3, 1986. Soon after birth, the infant showed signs of neonatal opiate withdrawal. A urine toxicology drug screen revealed the presence of heroin. The infant's neonatal opiate withdrawal was treated with phenobarbital, and she was released to Ann on January 13, 1986.

I interviewed Ann on January 16, 1986, at the request of Child Protective Services (CPS).

Drug History

Ann states that she started using heroin in December 1984. She denies skin popping (subcutaneous use) or intravenous use of heroin and says the route of administration was snorting. Ann says she snorted heroin every three to four days. In addition, she has been smoking pot since the age of thirteen. Ann admits to using cocaine and experimenting with other drugs such as LSD. She drinks beer with dinner, but states that heroin is her drug of choice and that it makes her feel the way she wants to feel.

Pregnancy History

Ann was on birth control pills but admits that she skipped her pills. She had light spotting one period, missed her next period, and was finally diagnosed as being ten weeks pregnant.

In June 1985, Ann went to the methadone program to detoxify from heroin. Her stay sounds unusual. She says she was placed on the twenty-one-day detox schedule and that the methadone made her extremely nauseated. She states she was so ill from the methadone that she could not get off it. She was then placed on methadone maintenance and took 10 milligrams a day. I questioned her as to why she went on methadone maintenance if her heroin addiction was so minimal and of such short duration. She had no answers to these questions.

It is difficult to understand why Ann continued on methadone if it made her this ill and if her heroin dose was indeed as low and as infrequent as she implies.

Ann was not a successful client on the methadone program. She continued to use heroin and showed up with five urines positive for heroin. She also had nine "administrative dirties" in which she refused to give urine for testing. These fourteen positive tests are excessive for any methadone client and should not have been tolerated in a pregnant woman.

Ann says that she stopped her methadone over Labor Day weekend and took heroin. She said she felt so "lousy and irritable" with her three-year-old daughter that she took heroin and felt much better.

Presently Ann says she is off methadone completely. She denies ever being arrested. She states she was never arrested for driving under the influence of drugs or alcohol and denies prior drug treatment.

Relationship with Infant

Ann had the infant with her during the interview. She is breast feeding the infant and demonstrates a warm and caring manner. She is aware that any drugs she takes will pass through the breast milk and could harm the baby.

She states that she saw the baby daily when she was in the hospital and made a point of feeding the baby herself. Although she was not permitted to breast feed the baby at first, Ann did pump her breasts to keep the milk coming in.

I would suggest that CPS question the nurses at the nursery in order to ascertain their opinion about the level of care and bonding demonstrated by Ann toward her infant.

Relationship with Baby's Father

Ann plans to marry Cary, the baby's father. Cary and she have lived together since her first child was three months old. Supposedly, Cary does not use heroin but does drink beer heavily.

Social-Family History

Ann describes herself as being rebellious in her youth. She dropped out of high school in her junior year and got a GED. She went to community college but never finished. Ann feels that she has been rebelling against her career-oriented parents.

Summary

There are clear indicators of strength in this case, but there are also reasons for concern. In defense of Ann's ability to care for the child is the fact that she did seek assistance for her heroin dependency, did not progress beyond snorting heroin as evidenced by the lack of needle marks in her anticubital fossae, admits that she has an "addictive personality," and appears willing to cooperate with a treatment plan.

Of concern is the fact that Ann's charming personality disarms treatment personnel and engages them in a manner that allows them to buy in to her minimizing her drug dependency. Five positive urines and nine administrative dirty urines should never have been tolerated and should have clued the methadone staff in to the fact that this pregnant woman was exposing her unborn infant to both methadone and heroin.

Her partner's alcohol use is also reason for concern. Ann will not be successful in developing abstinence from all psychoactive drugs and sobriety from alcohol while her partner drinks heavily. Since they are living together and plan to marry, the treatment plan should also include him.

Clearly, Ann does have some strengths on which to build a successful recovery program. It will be the responsibility of Child Protective Services, Public Health Nurses, and her drug treatment counselor to understand the depth of her addiction and not to buy into her "acting as if" everything is under control.

I recommend that Ann be involved with outpatient drug treatment counseling at Women's Crisis Support. In addition, both Cary and Ann should be involved with a minimum of three meetings a week of Alcoholics Anonymous and Narcotics Anonymous.

I believe that with an aggressive outpatient program and close coordination among CPS, Women's Crisis Support, the alcohol treatment program, the pediatrician, and Public Health Nurses, Ann does stand a good chance at recovery. Moreover, this level of supervision will be essential to protect the infant from further exposure to narcotics via the breast milk.

Please contact me should you have any further questions.

4
Strategies for AIDS Prevention

Motivating Health Behavior in Chemically Dependent Women

AIDS presents a major challenge to drug treatment programs. According to Ashery (1986), drug abuse treatment programs must become involved with combating the AIDS epidemic for the following reasons:

1. One of every four AIDS cases to date has been an intravenous drug user.

2. Contaminated needles are now, directly or indirectly, the major sources of this fatal disease for women, newborns, prisoners, and minorities.

3. AIDS cases linked to drug abuse are now spreading rapidly throughout the nation.

4. The potential for these numbers to increase is real.

5. The only hope for control of AIDS now is education and prevention because there is not yet any reliable cure or vaccine.

6. Intravenous (IV) drug users are hard to reach with AIDS prevention messages.

Furthermore, it is believed that AIDS prevention and education material will need to be specifically tailored to chemically dependent women in order for it to change their knowledge, attitude, and health behaviors. This chapter acquaints the reader with some of the basic issues concerning women and AIDS and with some intervention techniques that might be responsive to the particular needs of chemically dependent women.

Epidemiology

To date, women comprise a small percentage (7 percent) of AIDS cases—3,653 women versus 45,862 men (Centers for Disease Control 1988). The prevalence of AIDS among women is likely to increase, however, since the incidence of AIDS attributed to heterosexual contact is increasing, while the incidence of AIDS attributed to homosexual/bisexual contact is leveling off. The Centers for Disease Control (CDC) estimates that another 7,300 to 36,000 women have AIDS related complex (ARC) and that there are fifty to eighty times as many women who test positive for the human immunodeficiency virus (HIV) antibody as there are women with active cases of AIDS (at least 180,000 women).

According to figures from the CDC for 1988, women with AIDS come from the following risk groups:

	Number	Percent
IV drug users	1,843	50
Heterosexual contact	1,074	29
Transfusion recipients	395	11
Undetermined	251	9

While IV drug users make up the largest group of women at risk for AIDS, the sexual partners of IV drug users are the second largest group of at risk women. CDC figures show that of women who were infected with AIDS as the result of heterosexual contact, 69 percent had their heterosexual contact with an IV drug user (versus 16 percent with a bisexual).

The fourth largest group of women with AIDS falls into the CDC category of undetermined. It is believed that the women who fall into this category represent second generation transmission.

That is, their partners might not be in high-risk groups but might have had sex with others in a high-risk group. Many of the women in this group might be partners of men who are covering up their IV drug use, HIV seropositive results, or sexual practices.

While it is difficult to estimate the number of women IV drug users, it is imperative to recognize that a successful AIDS prevention/education effort must reach out aggressively to the following groups of women: IV drug users in treatment, IV drug users not in treatment, partners of IV drug users, workers in the sex industry (prostitutes).

IV Drug Users in Treatment

Female IV drug users who are in treatment should be seen as having needs unique from their male counterparts. Prevention, education, and intervention techniques should be tailored toward enhancing the self-efficacy and sense of self-esteem of these clients.

IV Drug Users Not in Treatment

It is estimated that for every chemically dependent person in treatment, there are seven who are not in treatment. Women, especially IV drug users, are underrepresented in traditional drug treatment programs. In addition, it is estimated that one-third of all prostitutes are also IV drug users.

Partners of IV Drug Users

It is reported that 80 percent of male IV drug users have their primary relationship with women who do not themselves use such drugs. As Des Jarlais et al. (1984) have reported, male IV drug users who test seropositive are typically not ready to disclose this information to their partners for fear of rejection and withdrawal of support. This cover-up poses a significant risk to women.

The non—drug using female partners of male IV drug users may well constitute the largest hidden population of women at risk for AIDS. These women may not know that their male partners are IV drug users, and they are difficult to reach because they are not associated with a treatment program.

Prostitutes

Women who work in the sex industry are at an increased risk of exposure to the AIDS virus based on a number of factors, including the following:

- Multiple sex partners
- Anonymous sex with partners who may be seropositive or who may fall into one of the high-risk groups
- High-risk sexual activity
- IV drug use
- Decreased vigilance about proper safe sex practices because of their use of alcohol or drugs

Cofactors That Increase a Woman's Risk for AIDS

Everyone who is exposed to the AIDS virus will not develop AIDS. In fact, researchers believe that the virulence of the AIDS virus depends on specific modes of transmission (that is, direct intimate contact with bodily fluids), repeated exposure over time, and preexisting or concurrent conditions in the host (cofactors). Unfortunately, many of the cofactors associated with AIDS are known to exist in drug users. These cofactors include poor nutrition, use of drugs known to suppress the immune system, repeated bouts of infections, and high stress.

Nutrition

Women heroin users frequently state that they use heroin to lose weight. Poor nutrition secondary to drug use is not just a by-product of poor eating habits but actually results from the direct appetite suppressant effect of the drug. In addition, alcohol is known to exert a direct toxic effect on the gastrointestinal tract; this leads to an impaired absorption of food. Malnutrition is further exacerbated by inadequate assimilation of vitamins and amino acids due to damaged liver cells.

In some women, chemical dependency coexists with anorexia nervosa or bulimia. It is common for women with eating disorders to attempt to control their perceived weight problem through the combined use of drugs and starvation. Ultimately, the body's immune system is compromised due to the chronic state of malnutrition.

Drugs

Drugs enhance an individual's risk for developing AIDS in multiple ways. Alcohol, nitrites (poppers), amphetamines, and marijuana are all known to suppress the body's immune system. Nitrites lead to a depletion of the helper T cells by directly injuring these cells. Nitrites also are known as cofactors in the development of various forms of cancer.

In addition, the use of drugs to enhance sex might make it difficult to practice safe sex. Drugs that cause muscle relaxation and blood vessel dilation might enhance the absorption of the virus into the bloodstream. Decreased judgment and decreased pain sensitivity also might make the participants less aware of the trauma involved in certain physical acts.

Infections

As discussed in chapter 1, women drug users complain of medical problems more often than do men drug users. Indeed, a medical complaint often precipitates a woman's entrance into drug treatment. Chemically dependent women are at increased risk for infections, anemia, sexually transmitted diseases, hepatitis, hypertension, diabetes, urinary tract infections, gynecological problems, and dental disease, including abscesses.

During drug treatment, women continue to experience more medical problems than their male counterparts. While this might reflect a sociocultural bias (that is, it is more acceptable for women to be medically ill), it also might reflect the fact that drugs exert a more toxic influence on women. There is growing evidence that this is certainly the case for alcohol (Wilsnack and Beckman 1984). In particular, these drug dependent women appear to be vulnerable to the traditional sexually transmitted diseases of gonorrhea, trichomonas, and chlamydia and the sequellae of exposure to these infections, which include pelvic inflammatory disease, chronic scarring of the fallopian tubes, decreased fertility, and increased abnormal cervical Pap tests. As a result of needle use or skin popping, IV drug using women also expose themselves to other infections, including abscesses, cellulitis, endocarditis, and hepatitis. For a detailed discussion of the medical needs of chemically dependent women, see Mondanaro 1981a and 1981b.

Stress

Chemically dependent women experience extremely high levels of stress as compared with both male drug users and non–drug using women. Areas of increased stress include responsibility for children, living alone, low income, low level of education, lack of financial resources, partners who use drugs, more dysfunction and pathology in the family of origin, higher levels of depression and anxiety, and lower levels of self-esteem (Reed 1981). In addition, chemically dependent women tend to score high on recent life change events, which are other stressors.

Prevention Motivation

Much of the AIDS prevention to date has occurred in the homosexual/bisexual male community. These prevention efforts appear to have been highly successful. One prospective study reported that 80 percent of the respondents had substantially changed their sexual behavior from November 1982 to May 1984 (Coates 1985). Included in these changes are significant decreases in the following high-risk behaviors:

- Number of new contacts
- Number of partners
- Receptive anal intercourse without condoms
- Oral-anal contact
- Swallowing semen

In addition, the number of rectal gonorrhea cases have declined by 75 percent in San Francisco since 1982. The San Francisco AIDS Foundation believes that this is a direct result of AIDS education.

Is it reasonable to expect similar prevention efforts to have such an equally positive effect on women who are chemically dependent? The response must be a resounding and pessimistic no. The demographics of this gay male population are diametrically opposed to the demographics of the female IV drug using group. These differences must be acknowledged and understood so that a prevention program can be developed that will be responsive to the unique needs of the chemically dependent woman.

One report of changes in sexual behavior of gay men in San Francisco studied 454 men with the following demographics: some college, 68 percent; white collar or professional work, 77 percent; mean reported income, $24,000 (Coates 1985). In comparison, studies of chemically dependent women demonstrate a level of unemployment that varies from 81 to 96 percent. Most chemically dependent women in federally funded treatment programs have not completed a high school education; even after completion of treatment, 72 percent of the women are still unemployed and lack the skills necessary for gainful employment (Sutker 1981).

The ethnic breakdown of AIDS cases is illustrated in the following chart:

	All Cases	Homosexual Men	Women
White	60%	74%	28%
Black	25%	15%	51%
Hispanic	14%	10%	21%

These statistics underscore the fact that ethnic minorities are overrepresented among women with AIDS (72 percent), as compared to homosexual men (25 percent) and all AIDS cases (39 percent).

In fact, the cumulative incidence of AIDS in black and Hispanic women is more than ten times that found in white women (Centers for Disease Control 1987a).

Motivation for Health Behaviors

To understand the complex nature of health behavior choices and motivators, we must turn to preventive medicine. As discussed in chapter 1, researchers in this field have learned that one's ability to utilize health education information and to make changes in one's behavior depends largely on socioeconomic status, educational level, sense of power, and vocation. Of all the variables that affect health behavior, socioeconomic status is considered the most influential. Health behavior and socioeconomic status are related through the following variables (Sandelowski 1981):

Family of origin: The family influences the value of its members.

Social participation: The more an individual interacts socially, the more she will be exposed to different health behaviors and beliefs.

Work self-direction: The more control an individual has over her work situation, the more control she may believe she has over other situations.

Sense of powerlessness: Lower socioeconomic status people experience feelings of powerlessness.

Health knowledge: upper socioeconomic status people are better informed about various health behaviors.

Belief in effectiveness: There is a positive correlation between income level and the belief that a health measure will be effective.

Empowering Techniques

To be effective, strategies for AIDS prevention and education with high-risk women must be based on empowering techniques. The process by which AIDS information is disseminated is as important as the content. The fear of contracting a fatal disease such as AIDS because of belonging to a high-risk group, coupled with the woman's sense of hopelessness and powerlessness, can be severely debilitating. Denying her vulnerability to AIDS or assuming the fatalistic attitude that she will contract the disease no matter what precautions she takes might be the woman's only defense. *defense*

Chemically dependent women often feel like second class citizens and are very sensitive to real or imagined messages that they are not worthy of help. It would be easy for such women to get the idea from AIDS prevention programs that they are being seen as unclean, potential spreaders of AIDS to more worthy members of society. It is important, therefore, to set any educational program about AIDS within the context of genuine concern for the well-being of the chemically dependent woman herself.

Didactic presentations will probably be the least effective method of reaching these women and bringing about both an increase in their knowledge and changes in their behavior. Methods that involve these women in the development and delivery of their own programs are more likely to be successful. Every client and community population contains individuals who are highly respected and recognized by other members of that identified group and make up an informal network of indigenous community helpers. These individuals can become an integral part of the community's educational efforts by bridging the gap between the formal organizations and the various targeted populations of high-risk women.

The techniques of activating clients and identifying natural helpers can be utilized within the drug treatment program, in jail and prison settings, with groups of women who work in the sex industry, and within the community at large. Information given by these trusted individuals will carry more weight than information given by counselors, jail guards, or other people who might not be perceived as having the women's well-being as their primary goal. Natural helpers can be identified and selected from all the groups of women a program wishes to reach. Depending on the location and situation, target groups might be broken down by drug of choice (IV speed users, IV heroin users, and so on), ethnicity, area of residence, or any other category that reflects the natural affinity of the targeted women. The following steps can be used in establishing such a program:

1. Identify affinity groups within the high-risk groups of women.

2. Gather input from the natural helpers as to the concerns of the women in their subgroups.

3. Design an educational program with input from the natural helpers.

4. Select teams of natural helpers from each targeted group.

5. Train the teams in both the content and process areas of AIDS education.

6. Assist the teams in providing drop-in groups and educational forums for their particular target populations.

7. Offer ongoing support and backup to the teams of natural helpers.

Basically, this is a training of trainers model that utilizes trusted members of the community's informal networks.

The formal drug programs and other community organizations can offer space for meetings, printed educational material, resource lists, and other tangible support for the informal networking being carried out by the natural helpers.

COYOTE, Call off Your Old Tired Ethics, the national organization for women in the sex industry, has written its own guidelines for AIDS prevention. In addition, it holds open meetings called The Bad Girls Rap Group during which women can discuss their concerns and have their questions answered in a supportive, nonthreatening environment. This type of organizing builds on the strengths found in a particular group. For example, women who work in the sex industry often practice safe sex and are very knowledgeable about techniques for avoiding sexually transmitted diseases. These skills can be acknowledged and used to teach women who might not be as familiar with safe sex practices.

It is imperative that drug programs assist women in taking control of their own lives. A prevention strategy that empowers and activates women is also a good treatment strategy. While the rest of this training segment focuses primarily on content, it should be remembered that the process by which a program reaches women will be the difference between success and failure.

Education and Outreach

Education and outreach to prevent the transmission of AIDS will require a multilevel approach involving a variety of organizations that provide services to women. Women at risk can be reached through the following agencies: public health departments, family planning clinics, social service agencies, city and county jails, state prisons, women's health centers, battered women's shelters, women's crisis programs, and drug treatment programs.

Service agency staff and members of the at-risk groups should be trained to give the training themselves. Specific strategies that have been used to reach women include the following (Shaw 1985):

Outreach to health providers

Development of an advocacy and information network of women working on AIDS issues

Direct media advertising

Use of existing community institutions, including health, social services, ethnic, religious, and other cultural organizations

Material development in appropriate languages, including incorporating AIDS information into existing materials, such as those concerning sexually transmitted diseases

Hot lines, mass media education, and multiethnic outreach programs

Talking about Sex

How to avoid being infected if you are not, how to avoid further infection if you have already been exposed, and how to avoid infecting others all entail the same practices. The main point is to keep the message simple. Women might be experiencing some neurological deficits secondary to drug use, as well as decreased attentiveness due to anxiety. Repetition of simple messages reinforced with printed material will help get the information across.

In this culture we have very few words to adequately discuss sex and body parts. Vocabulary is limited to scientific medical jargon, streetwise "dirty" words, or baby talk. It is imperative that the words selected are understood by all and that street talk not be avoided because of the counselor's discomfort or embarrassment. At the same time, the counselor must communicate a sense of respect and dignity while utilizing common terms. A counselor must not take for granted that everyone understands what she or he is saying. Clients might be too embarrassed to admit that they do not understand a certain term or activity.

Counselors are often uncomfortable when dealing with issues of sexuality, and special training should be offered to prepare the staff for this. For a more detailed discussion of counselor attitudes, training, and resources in the area of sexuality and intimacy, see Mondanaro et al. 1982.

Safe and Unsafe Sex Practices

 Both medical and common terms will be used here to describe safe and unsafe sex practices. Women need to understand that the AIDS virus is transmitted through direct contact with infected bodily fluids: blood, semen, urine, feces, and vaginal secretions, including menstrual blood. Although the virus is found in saliva and tears, it is not believed to be at a high enough level to cause transmission.

Safe sex involves the avoidance of activities in which there is tissue trauma or an exchange of bodily fluids. Until recently, sex practices have been characterized as safe, possibly safe, and unsafe in regard to AIDS transmission. Research has recently documented that latex condoms prevent the transmission of the AIDS virus. As a result of these findings, AIDS educators are attempting to narrow the categories to two, safe and unsafe sex practices. This simplification will make it easier for chemically dependent women to understand the guidelines.

Safe Sex

Safe sex includes activities that involve only skin-to-skin contact, where there are no breaks in the skin from sores, infections, or wounds. Some of these activities are massage; hugging; body-to-body rubbing (frottage); social (dry) kissing; voyeurism, exhibitionism, or fantasy; touching your own genitals (masturbation); and using your own sex toys (do not share sex toys).

Using condoms, latex gloves, and latex barriers to avoid exchanging bodily fluids is safe as long as they are used properly and do not come off or break. The proper use of these protective devices will allow the couple to engage safely in the following sexual activities: vaginal intercourse (with a condom), fellatio (with a condom), cunnilingus (with a latex barrier), hand/finger-to-genital contact (with latex gloves).

It is advised that women use spermicidal jellies and creams with condoms as a backup method in case the condom slips, breaks, or falls off. Nonoxynol-9, the active ingredient in spermicides, has been found to kill the AIDS virus in a laboratory dish and is known to provide some protection from other sexually transmitted diseases, such as gonorrhea. Spermicides can be placed inside the tip of the condom. Make sure you are using a spermicide and not a lubricant. Some women, especially women who work in the sex industry, have learned to put a condom on the male partner with their mouth. This has helped to protect them while performing fellatio. It is advised, though, that the woman put the condom on her partner with her hand and not her mouth.

Disposable latex gloves can be purchased at any dental or surgical supply house. The latex barrier (rubber dam) is a thin piece of latex that is the same thickness as a physician's disposable glove. Latex barriers come in rolls or sheets and can also be purchased at dental and surgical supply houses. Cunnilingus is performed by placing the latex barrier between the tongue and vulva. Like condoms, latex gloves and/or latex barriers must be thrown away and not reused.

Basically, educators are attempting to change the community norm so that using condoms becomes the norm. For heterosexual women to practice safe sex, they must convince their male partners to wear condoms. Male counselors can model appropriate behavior for the male clients by supporting and encouraging the use of condoms. *Condom Sense* is a very good film that can be shown to both men and women in drug treatment programs. While it was not developed for AIDS prevention, it provides basic information about the use of condoms and the myth of decreased sensitivity. It presents material in a humorous and entertaining fashion, which affects the attitudes of both men and women. See the resource list at the back of the book for information regarding the availability of this film.

Unsafe Sex

Unsafe sex is basically any activity that allows the direct contact of bodily fluids, including vaginal or anal intercourse without a condom, semen or urine in the mouth, fellatio without a condom, blood contact of any kind (including menstrual blood), oral-anal contact, hand in the rectum or vagina, sharing of sex toys, and being too stoned to know what is safe. Sharing needles is always unsafe, no matter what an individual's sexual practices. Some health educators believe that anal intercourse causes so much trauma and tissue damage and is such a high-risk activity that it should not be done even with condoms.

Changing Sexual Behaviors

Practicing safe sex might pose a substantial challenge for chemically dependent women. These women are being asked to change both their drug taking behaviors and their sexual behaviors. Many chemically dependent women already experience difficulty in the area of sexuality. For some women, sexuality is the only way they know to experience intimacy. Drug programs must appreciate the core changes that are being demanded of these women. In addition, women might be afraid to tell their partners that they need to change their sexual practices because they fear rejection and abandonment.

Despite a hardened exterior, these women are often exceptionally passive as a result of strict sex role socialization. They have learned that to be feminine means to be passive and nonassertive. These women often test at the extreme end of feminine, while their chemically dependent male partners test at the extreme end of masculine. The result is that the woman might be too passive to exert herself and the man might not accept his responsibility or cooperate in sexual risk reduction. Some male partners refused to practice safe sex because they believed these changes to be unmasculine.

Drug programs must assist chemically dependent women to escape from this socially passive role. Women role models will be extremely important in getting across the message that a woman must take responsibility for her own body. Natural helpers can be of great assistance in modeling assertive behavior and in giving these women permission to do things differently. For example, women who work in the sex industry could be invited to discuss safe sex practices.

Anticipating a woman's hesitation and discomfort, providing support, and creating opportunities for role playing all help increase her confidence. Warnings about AIDS can be misinterpreted to mean that these women should not have any fun or pleasure in their lives. Frank discussion about how to enjoy sex and keep it safe at the same time is necessary. These sessions will be more believable if the information is presented by individuals who truly believe that safe sex can be fully satisfying and enjoyable.

It is imperative for all women who are IV drug users, partners of IV drug users, or prostitutes or who have sex with anonymous or multiple partners to practice safe sex. Material regarding testing and seropositivity might confuse the simple message that all women in these high-risk groups must receive. One very powerful newspaper ad summed up the message this way: Practice Safe Sex for Life.

HIV Antibody Testing

In November 1985, 728 homosexual and bisexual men were surveyed as to whether or not they would voluntarily be tested for the

HIV antibody if the test were available free of charge (Coates 1985). The majority (69 percent) said that they would get the test. Among the individuals who said that they would not get tested, the most common reason was a concern about confidentiality. It is also interesting to note that the desire to be tested for the antibody was significantly higher among individuals who believed that they had not been exposed to the AIDS virus. Fewer of the individuals who believed that they were incubating the virus wanted to be tested.

If a woman believes that she has been exposed to and is currently harboring the AIDS virus, she might not want to be tested. Again, denial is a very strong defense. At a time when AIDS hysteria is high, it is important that programs carefully think through plans for HIV antibody testing. Insurance companies are threatening not to cover individuals who test positive for the virus; some employers are threatening not to hire individuals who test positive. A record of a positive test might have a serious detrimental effect on an individual's ability to earn a living. This can be particularly devastating to women who are already locked out of the mainstream of society. This is a time for drug programs to be vigilant in the areas of client confidentiality and client advocacy. Programs must be very clear about whom they are serving.

It is imperative for programs to maximize the benefits involved in HIV antibody testing and to minimize the potential harm that might result from disclosing the results. The following are offered as guidelines in this area:

1. Clients should be fully informed about what HIV seropositive or seronegative testing means, anonymity, and confidentiality prior to agreeing to the HIV test.

2. HIV antibody testing should be done voluntarily and confidentially.

3. Clients should be given anonymous testing in which each is assigned a number for her blood sample and her name is not recorded.

4. Thought should be given prior to noting positive results in the client's file.

Testing is a potentially powerful tool. It can give the individual immediate feedback on her status and might be an added incentive in following safe sex practices and avoiding the sharing of needles. The following must be explained to women who test negative:

1. A negative test does not mean they are immune to the virus.

2. They must still practice safe sex and avoid sharing needles.

3. They must be wary of feelings of invulnerability, which might make them less vigilant in the future.

4. They are still vulnerable to future exposure.

Chemically dependent women need to know that they must always practice safe sex and avoid using needles no matter what the result of their HIV antibody tests.

Pregnancy and AIDS

According to the CDC, 80 percent of pediatric AIDS cases are attributed to transmission from an infected parent (Centers for Disease Control 1987b). In 90 percent of these cases, the babies' mothers either used drugs intravenously or had male sexual partners who used IV drugs. Ethnic minority children comprise 80 percent of all pediatric AIDS cases (Centers for Disease Control 1986). The bulk of these cases represent in utero transmission. The AIDS virus also is found in breast milk. One infant in Australia is thought to have contracted the disease through the breast milk of her mother, who was exposed to the virus via a blood transfusion after delivery. Another potential source for contracting the virus is artificial insemination. Lesbians and other women who received donor semen are being followed in a San Francisco study to see whether they have developed antibodies to the HIV virus.

Chemically dependent women have been told that they should be tested for the AIDS virus prior to pregnancy. This is good advice but ignores the reality that most pregnant addicts do not plan their pregnancies. A lack of periods (amenorrhea) as a result of heroin use or decreased fertility as a result of repeated bouts of pelvic inflammatory disease make some chemically dependent women believe that they cannot get pregnant. Other women are too preoccupied with drugs to even think about the possibility of pregnancy or the need for contraception.

Contraceptive information must be made a major component of any AIDS prevention/education program for women. This should include the evaluation of women who falsely believe that they cannot get pregnant because they have scarring secondary to infections in the fallopian tubes. These women might have diminished fertility because of heroin use, but once they enter treatment and become abstinent from heroin, their fertility increases.

Pregnancy is associated with a suppression of immunity, particularly cell-mediated immunity. This is especially true during the last three months of pregnancy and is evident up to three months after delivery. It is known that this decreased immunity increases a woman's susceptibility to certain infections, and it is believed that it can make a pregnant woman more vulnerable to developing AIDS, especially if she is already seropositive (Centers for Disease Control 1985a).

What All Women Clients Should Know

All women in high-risk groups, regardless of their HIV antibody status, should receive information about AIDS. The following recommendations should be considered when presenting AIDS information to women clients:

1. Because of the high rate of dropout from drug treatment programs, information should be presented at intake and orientation.

2. Material should be presented in small, safe, all-women groups.

3. To avoid stigmatizing certain groups, sessions should be mandatory for all women.

4. A counselor/natural helper team should lead the groups to

help build a sense of trust and comfort among the participants.

All women should receive the following basic information about AIDS:

1. A fundamental description of AIDS

2. A discussion of the iceberg concept, which explains that AIDS represents only the end of a continuum that also includes HIV seropositivity and AIDS related conditions (ARC)

3. The fact that healthy people can be carriers of AIDS and that an IV drug user's physical appearance does not convey whether or not he is contagious for AIDS

4. How they can become infected (IV drug use—sharing needles, sex with IV drug users, sex with a man whose history they do not know, or sex with multiple partners)

5. That AIDS is not spread by casual contact

Women also need to know the following things about pregnancy and AIDS:

1. Seventy-three percent of pediatric AIDS is attributed to maternal transmission during pregnancy.

2. A seropositive woman does not need to be sick with the disease of AIDS to pass the disease on to her fetus.

3. Fifty to 60 percent of children born to seropositive mothers will be infected.

4. There is no way to prevent the fetus from becoming infected if the mother is infected.

5. Infants and children of seropositive mothers must be carefully monitored because the patient might not exhibit symptoms immediately at birth.

6. Pregnancy is a stress on the woman's body and as such

can increase the chances of an HIV infected woman's developing symptoms.

7. Seropositive women should not get pregnant.

8. High-risk women should get an HIV antibody test prior to getting pregnant.

9. The virus is passed in the breast milk, and seropositive women should avoid breast feeding.

10. Women in high-risk groups who do become pregnant should get the HIV antibody test.

What HIV Antibody Positive Women Should Know

Women who are seropositive but have no symptoms should be given the following information:

1. Regular medical evaluations and follow-up are advised.

2. They are probably infected for life.

3. They are probably contagious for life.

4. They must act as if they are contagious.

5. They cannot assume that they will or will not develop AIDS.

6. Persons who have been exposed to the seropositive woman—sexual partners, children, and persons with whom needles have been shared—should be offered HIV testing.

7. Repeated exposure to the virus can increase the chances of developing AIDS.

8. They should not have unsafe sex or share needles with other seropositive individuals.

9. Health maintenance efforts, including proper nutrition, abstinence and sobriety, stress management, safe sex prac-

tices, and no sharing of needles, can decrease the risk of seropositivity developing into ARC or AIDS.

10. They should not get pregnant.

11. They should use a reliable method of birth control.

12. They should not donate blood, plasma, body organs, or other tissue.

13. When seeking medical or dental care, they should inform health-care providers of their positive antibody status so that appropriate care can be given and precautions taken to prevent transmission.

It is important to stress the hope inherent in this situation and how women can avoid moving along the continuum from seropositivity to ARC to AIDS. Women must be made to realize that the exposure to the virus as represented by a positive antibody test does not mean that she will inevitably get AIDS. There is much she can do to increase her health status. Support groups should be initiated for women who are seropositive. Aside from answering questions and providing emotional support, these groups can focus on the tangible changes the women can and must make. Checklists, charts, diaries, or journals can be used to give the women a concrete record of health maintenance and behavioral changes they need to make. An example of a journal detailing problems and appropriate treatment is given in table 4–1. This or a similar format can be used to outline goals and objectives in the areas of stress management; relations with partners, family, and children; sobriety and abstinence, including involvement in Narcotics Anonymous and Alcoholics Anonymous; and financial planning.

The more specific a plan is, the more likely an individual is to accomplish her stated goals. Overall goals must be accompanied by discrete, measurable objectives that specify a time for completion. For example, a woman who is anemic might be told to take two iron pills with meals three times a day. Her diary would include the specific plan and a checklist to show whether or not this was accomplished.

Table 4–1
Sample Treatment Journal

Problem	Action Plan	Date
Health		
Identify health problems.	Get a complete physical exam.	
Resolve health problems.		
Anemia	Take iron three times daily.	
Pregnancy	Discuss with health worker.	
	Select birth control method.	
	List method here.	
	Use selected method.	
Nutrition		
Improve nutritional status.	See nutritionist.	
	Get a balanced diet.	
	Start a new diet.	

Problem	Action Plan		Mon.	Tues.	Wed.	Thurs.	Fri.	Sat.	Sun.
Anemia	Iron pills								
	2 at breakfast								
	2 at lunch								
	2 at dinner								

Weekly reviews of diaries will help these women stay on track and provide immediate positive feedback, as well as immediate assistance in problem areas. Start with areas in which the women can experience high rewards and low stress. Build on these positive experiences. As new women enter the group, the more experienced women will serve as role models.

Women need assistance in discussing their HIV status with partners. Anticipating their discomfort assists them in acquiring new skills for coping with this sensitive area. Encouraging role playing and having women share how they have told their partners will give the women opportunities to practice various approaches and find out what feels most comfortable. The program can facilitate this communication by offering couple counseling and group counseling for partners of seropositive clients.

These women also should be given the following information about their children and household activities:

1. The virus is not spread through casual contact such as coughing, sneezing, or sharing cups, telephones, or toilets.

2. They cannot "give AIDS" to anyone in the course of normal homemaking.

3. They can and should continue to hug their kids.

4. They can continue to cook and clean with normal attention to safety.

5. They should not share toothbrushes, razors, or other implements that could become contaminated with blood.

6. After accidents that result in bleeding, contaminated surfaces should be cleaned with household bleach freshly diluted with water (one part bleach to ten parts water).

7. Tampons and sanitary napkins should be disposed of carefully, since menstrual blood does contain the virus. (Centers for Disease Control 1985b)

Care of the Chemically Dependent Woman with AIDS

The primary care for the chemically dependent woman with AIDS may be the responsibility of medical personnel and the hospital staff. The drug treatment program will be part of a multidisciplinary team that involves many organizations, including the hospital, child protective services, human resources agencies, and public health departments.

Chemically dependent women most likely will not have the resources to develop the strong support networks seen in the gay community. For this reason, formal organizations will be an essential and primary provider of support for these women. In addition, plans must be made for dependent children prior to a woman's becoming too debilitated to care for them. Drug programs and other agencies may well serve as the lifeline for these women. It is imperative for the well-being of these women, their children, and the rest of society that the women not slip through the cracks that exist between various service providers.

5

Benzodiazepine Dependency and Detoxification

The Consequences of Misprescribing

Benzodiazepines (Valium-type drugs) were introduced to the public twenty-five years ago when chlordiazepoxide (Librium) became available to physicians. Although benzodiazepines were first synthesized in 1933, they did not undergo preclinical and clinical testing until the 1950s. The introduction of benzodiazepines was heralded as a new era in the treatment of anxiety.

In fact, the search for drugs to control nervous tension or anxiety has had a long history, beginning in the 1800s with the introduction of bromide salts. As is frequently the case with new psychoactive medications, the bromides were quite popular until their intoxication potential was appreciated.

In the early 1900s, the bromides were replaced by barbiturates. These drugs were initially regarded as safe and effective, but their ability to create tolerance and addiction was eventually noted. In addition, the barbiturates were implicated in lethal overdoses and suicides. The doses of barbiturates that were effective against anxiety also were capable of causing severe central nervous system depression and, in turn, mental impairment. The margin of safety between the effective dose and the lethal dose was ultimately seen as too narrow.

In the mid-1950s, the propanediol carbamates (meprobamate, Miltown, Equinil) were introduced as drugs whose major mode of action was anxiolytic. Unlike the barbiturates, whose antianxiety properties came about as a by-product of sedation, meprobamate was supposedly a dedicated anxiolytic—that is, a medication that directly affected anxiety. Time ultimately demonstrated that the carbamates were much more similar to the barbiturates than originally thought and that the antianxiety effects of these drugs were a by-product of central nervous system depression. Tolerance and dependence also develop with these drugs.

In comparison to these agents, benzodiazepines offered clear advantages in the treatment of anxiety. The two most important advantages were their greater specificity of action and their wider margin of safety. The initial belief that tolerance and dependence would not develop with these new drugs was, however, proven erroneous over time. Unfortunately, physicians, relieved to have alternatives to the lethal barbiturates, have had a difficult time appreciating some of the risks involved in the use of benzodiazepines. Radcliffe et al. (1985) provide a more detailed discussion of the pharmacology of psychoactive drugs for the non–medically trained reader.

Use of Benzodiazepines

Benzodiazepines are now used for the following situations: short-term treatment of sleep disorders, short-term and intermittent treatment of anxiety, treatment for severe agitation and panic, short- and long-term treatment of seizure disorders, and as premedicants before surgical or diagnostic procedures. While benzodiazepines were developed as antianxiety drugs to be used for mental disorders, the majority of the prescriptions for them are written by general practitioners and internists and are given for medical rather than mental disorders (Friedel 1985; Parry et al. 1973). One study demonstrated that general practitioners prescribed this category of drugs more frequently than any other (Skegg et al. 1977).

One hundred million prescriptions were written for benzodiazepines in 1973 and 70 million prescriptions were written in 1984, with approximately twice as many women as men receiving these prescriptions (Friedel 1985). Currently, "it is estimated that approximately 40 million doses of benzodiazepine drugs are consumed worldwide each day, with over 2 billion tablets of diazepam (Valium) alone prescribed in the United States during the course of a single year" (Lader 1985a, 25). In fact, the use of benzodiazepines has become so widespread that it has been termed a "mass cultural phenomenon" (Bellantuono et al. 1980).

Adverse Effects of Benzodiazepine Use

Adverse effects of benzodiazepines fall into three categories: central nervous system depression, potentiation of alcohol and other drugs, and paradoxical and other effects. These are explained in detail below.

Central Nervous System Depression

Central nervous system (CNS) depression caused by benzodiazepines can cause the following symptoms:

- Daytime somnolence (sleepiness)
- Motor weakness and fatigue
- Motor incoordination
- Decreased cognition (thinking)
- Decreased manual dexterity
- Cerebellar symptoms

> Nystagmus (involuntary rapid eye movement)
> Dysarthria (imperfect articulation of speech)
> Ataxia (inability to coordinate voluntary bodily movements)
> Disinhibition of anger

- Rebound insomnia

Patients taking even normal therapeutic doses have been noted to experience diazepam toxicity, which includes "depression, apprehension, tremulousness, insomnia and suicidal ideation. The patients, none of whom had a history of psychiatric disorders, were taking 40 mg or more of diazepam daily. There are several reports of diazepam-associated self-destructive ideation, which has led to successful suicide in a few cases" (Lader 1985a, 27). Individuals receiving even low doses of benzodiazepines experience learning difficulties and memory impairment.

Potentiation of Alcohol and Other Drugs

According to a study by the National Institute on Drug Abuse (NIDA), in 1984 "alcohol and diazepam accounted for more emergency room visits due to ingestion of two or more drugs than did any other agents" (Lader 1985a, 29). This is a particularly dangerous combination because alcohol enhances the absorption of benzodiazepines. Alcohol can potentiate the CNS depressant effect of benzodiazepines, even if the alcohol is ingested a day after the nocturnal use of the benzodiazepine.

Paradoxical and Other Effects

Sometimes the benzodiazepines have effects that are opposite from the anticipated outcomes. The following side effects (Lader 1985a) occur less frequently than those mentioned above:

- Depression
- Confusion
- Excitement
- Extreme talkativeness
- Increased anxiety
- Increased hostility
- Agitation
- Toxic psychosis
- Paranoid reactions
- Hypomanic and manic reactions
- Aggressive outbursts
- Rage reactions

Acute Overdose

Severe CNS depression is the hallmark of acute benzodiazepine overdose. The symptoms include:

- Slurred speech
- Staggering gait
- Sustained nystagmus
- Slowed reactions
- Lethargy
- Progressive respiratory depression

If there is enough CNS depression, the patient might be stuporous to comatose, and the following lifesaving measures will be necessary: maintenance of airway, assisted respiration, cardiovascular support, and gastric lavage.

Benzodiazepine Dependency

Research has shown that all benzodiazepines except the long-acting flurazepam (Dalmane) are ineffective against insomnia after fourteen consecutive nights of drug administration. Sleep specialist Kales says that physicians go wrong by prescribing these drugs for months without referring the patient for psychotherapy (Kales et al. 1982; Kales and Kales 1984).

Benzodiazepines are similarly misprescribed for the long-term treatment of anxiety.

> The Committee on the Review of Medicines in the United Kingdom noted that there was little evidence to suggest that benzodiazepines were effective in the management of anxiety beyond four months. Since data on prescribing practices reveal that benzodiazepines account for repeat prescriptions more than any other class of drugs, it has become increasingly apparent that factors other than therapeutic efficacy may be motivating patients to prolong drug use. Although long-term benzodiazepine treatment certainly reflects both the prevalence and potential chronicity of anxiety states, the possibility that many of these refilled prescriptions signal some process of dependence cannot be summarily dismissed. (Lader 1985a, 26)

The indiscriminate and long-term use of benzodiazepines for the treatment of anxiety and insomnia may well be creating one of the largest groups of chemically dependent people. Lader postulates that there may be as many as one million individuals in the United States who take benzodiazepines for long periods of time solely because they are physically dependent on the drugs. He believes that these individuals should be gradually withdrawn from the drugs and their cases reviewed in order to provide optimum care (Lader 1985b).

Benzodiazepine Withdrawal Syndrome

There has been much controversy about the subject of benzodiazepine withdrawal, especially in the following areas: low-dose versus high-dose withdrawal syndrome, symptom reemergence versus withdrawal syndrome, and physicians' reluctance to diagnose benzodiazepine withdrawal syndrome. These topics are discussed below.

Low-Dose versus High-Dose Withdrawal Syndrome

As previously noted, when the benzodiazepines were first marketed twenty-five years ago, physicians believed that tolerance and dependence would not develop. Gradually they recognized that individuals who were taking high doses—that is, above the usually prescribed quantities—were experiencing a withdrawal syndrome.

Over time it was learned that the withdrawal syndrome occurs not only after the cessation of a high-dose chronic use of benzodiazepines, but also after discontinuation of low to moderate doses of the drugs; that is, routinely used doses, of whatever size, lead to an abstinence syndrome.

> Most troubling is the fact that these symptoms have not differed qualitatively or quantitatively from those evidenced in patients withdrawn from high-dose therapy. It can be conjectured that one reason why chronic users of even moderate doses of benzodiazepines experience difficulty in stopping medication is the development of withdrawal symptoms. This may explain why so many repeat prescriptions are issued despite the paucity of adequate clinical evidence establishing long-term efficacy. (Lader 1985a, 31)

In addition, whether the drug is stopped abruptly or the dosage is gradually decreased, the patient will still experience some symptoms of withdrawal, although these symptoms are considerably less severe if the individual is tapered off the drug very slowly (Lader 1985a). A more detailed discussion of benzodiazepine detoxification is presented later in this chapter.

Symptom Reemergence versus Withdrawal Syndrome

While some researchers have stated that the patient experiences symptom reemergence rather than a withdrawal syndrome after the cessation of benzodiazepine use, Lader disagrees. "Although the symptoms that many patients experience on reduction or withdrawal of their benzodiazepine drug appear at first to resemble anxiety, it is our impression that they are in fact qualitatively different from the original symptoms for which benzodiazepine treatment was prescribed. Also, the perceptual symptoms characteristic of withdrawal are not typically found in anxiety itself" (Lader 1985a, 32).

Physicians' Reluctance to Diagnose Withdrawal Syndrome

Physicians have been and continue to be reluctant to recognize benzodiazepine withdrawal. In one study, physicians were asked to evaluate twenty-four patients who, unknown to them, were going through a benzodiazepine withdrawal. These physicians stated that seventeen out of the twenty-four were indeed experiencing a withdrawal syndrome. When the physicians learned that the patients were on diazepam, "their evaluations underwent modification, and they perceived less addiction in these same patients. The authors concluded that physicians tend to discount the significance of withdrawal-like symptoms when the drug in question is diazepam" (Lader 1985a, 32).

Clinical Withdrawal Symptoms

Benzodiazepine abstinence syndrome is divided into groups of symptoms. Symptoms that are not life threatening are called *minor,* but this term is quite misleading because there is nothing minor about the pain and suffering individuals experience from the withdrawal of these drugs. Symptoms that can cause death are called *major*.

Non–life-threatening (minor) symptoms include the following:

- Dysphoria
- Anxiety
- Panic
- Tachycardia (increased heart rate) and palpitations
- Increased blood pressure
- Impaired memory and concentration
- Irritability
- Insomnia
- Nightmares
- Agitation
- Muscle twitching, tremors
- Gastrointestinal problems, stomach cramps
- Anorexia, nausea
- Weight loss
- Increased sensitivity to light and sound
- Malaise, lack of energy
- Paresthesias (changes in sense of touch)
- Metallic taste

Life-threatening (major) symptoms include the following:

- Hyperpyrexia (increased body temperature)
- Grand mal seizures
- Psychosis
- Delirium

The particular benzodiazepine used will dictate the type of withdrawal syndrome. The primary distinction is whether the benzodiazepine falls into the long-acting or short-acting category. The duration of action for the benzodiazepines is outlined in table 5–1.

Long-acting benzodiazepines have the following characteristics:

Table 5–1

Duration of Action for Benzodiazepines

Generic Name	Trade Name	Plasma Half-Life	Daily Average Therapeutic Range
Very short acting			
Triazolam	Halcion	2 to 6 hours	0.25 to 0.5 mg.
Short acting			
Alprazolam	Xanax	6 to 20 hours	0.5 to 4 mg.
Lorazepam	Ativan	9 to 22 hours	1 to 10 mg.
Oxazepam	Serax	6 to 24 hours	10 to 30 mg.
Temazepam	Restoril	5 to 20 hours	15 to 30 mg.
Intermediate acting			
Chlordiazepoxide	Librium	7 to 46 hours	15 to 100 mg.
Intermediate to long acting			
Diazepam	Valium	14 to 90 hours	4 to 40 mg.
Long acting			
Clorazepate	Tranxene	30 to 200 hours	7.5 to 60 mg.
Halazepam	Paxipam	30 to 200 hours	60 to 160 mg.
Prazepam	Centrax	30 to 200 hours	10 to 60 mg.
Very long acting			
Flurazepam	Dalmane	90 to 200 hours	15 to 30 mg.

complicated metabolic pathways, prolonged elimination times, active metabolites with a prolonged half-life, a gradual tapering effect, withdrawal symptoms that begin after three to four days, and less severe withdrawal symptoms. Short-acting benzodiazepines are characterized by more rapid elimination, no active metabolites, no tapering effect, withdrawal symptoms that begin immediately upon cessation, and more severe withdrawal symptoms.

I have found that one of the major problems involved in identifying and treating benzodiazepine withdrawal is that women often do not connect their dysphoric feeling with drug cessation, since their symptoms might not appear until days after ingestion of the last dose. Instead, women typically interpret these dysphoric feelings as indications of mental illness and an inability to cope. If medication is begun again and Valium, Tranxene, or Xanax stops these unpleasant feelings, this is misinterpreted as proof that the woman is indeed unbalanced and needs the medication. The woman, her family, and often her own physician are unaware that she is experiencing a withdrawal syndrome brought on by physical dependency on the drug.

Diazepam (Valium) withdrawal represents the prototype for long-acting benzodiazepine abstinence syndrome. There is typically a delayed onset of symptoms as follows:

Days 1–3 May feel fine

Days 3–4 Increased restlessness
           Agitation
           Headaches
           Difficulty eating
           Insomnia

Days 4–6 Increases in all the above symptoms plus the following symptoms:
              Muscle twitching in face and arms
              Metallic taste
              Skin feels as if it is on fire

Days 6–7 Increases in all the above symptoms plus the following symptom:
              Seizures

Benzodiazepine Detoxification

Abrupt cessation of benzodiazepines should be avoided since this will precipitate a severe abstinence syndrome. Individuals on low to moderate doses should be tapered off the medication slowly, even if they have been on it for only a few months. Individuals on acute high doses also should be tapered off the medication slowly. While this detoxification can begin in a hospital program, the typical twenty-eight-day inpatient program is not long enough for the slow withdrawal that is necessary. A lowering of tolerance can be accomplished during an in-hospital stay, but the tapering off should continue slowly in an outpatient setting. The following should be obtained or performed prior to initiating the detoxification process:

• Detailed drug history

- Permission to contact prescribing physicians and pharmacists
- Comprehensive medical workup, including urine analysis for toxicology
- Commitment to therapy
- Design of schedule for slow detoxification

A plan for slow detoxification should include these elements:

1. Make sure the patient stops alcohol and cocaine use immediately.

2. Prescribe AA, NA, or Cocaine Anonymous (CA) meetings.

3. Decrease benzodiazepine dose by one-sixth every seven to ten days.

4. Anticipate that withdrawal will take two to three months.

5. Schedule rationally divided doses based on the pharmacokinetics of the drug.

6. Design a detox contract with client input.

7. Prescribe small quantities at a time.

8. Use only one pharmacy.

9. Do not permit refills.

10. Require therapy sessions one to three times weekly.

11. Separate drug use from emotional problems.

It is important not to increase the dose when the patient experiences difficult life situations. Instead offer increased therapy sessions, a nutritional consultation, an exercise plan, biofeedback, and guidance in relaxation or autohypnosis. Some programs prefer to substitute long-acting benzodiazepines for short-acting drugs during detoxification. Other programs substitute an equivalent dose of phenobarbital for the benzodiazepine and then slowly reduce the phenobarbital dosage. Many programs use the same benzodiazepine on which the individual is dependent for the detoxification. The approaches vary depending on the experience of the clinicians, the program setting, and the client population.

Proper Assessment of Anxiety and Insomnia

With proper assessment of anxiety and insomnia and institution of appropriate treatment measures, physicians could avoid creating chemical dependency in many clients. Likewise, it is imperative that clinicians withdrawing clients from benzodiazepines have a solid understanding of anxiety and insomnia. A more detailed presentation of these two extremely common complaints seems appropriate at this juncture.

Anxiety

Fear is a rational response to a real external threat. Low levels of anxiety can motivate an individual and therefore serve a very adaptive purpose. Beyond a certain point, however, anxiety becomes maladaptive. Anxiety is one of the more prevalent complaints brought to physicians, as it is believed to affect "an estimated one-third to one-half of all patients visiting a family physician" (Rickels 1985, 3).

Anxiety can be interpreted as a "normal" or nonpathological emotional response or as a symptom of a medical disorder. Between 10 and 40 percent of patients who present with anxiety do have an underlying physical illness that is causing the anxiety. These disorders include endocrine problems, such as thyroid dysfunction; cardiovascular disorders, such as mitral valve prolapse; pulmonary problems, such as asthma and pneumonia; and infectious disorders, such as colitis (Klerman 1985).

Anxiety also can be a symptom of drug effects, resulting from the use of legal prescriptions. Many commonly used medications can cause anxiety. These include antihypertensives, steroids, and nonsteroidal antiinflammatory drugs. In addition, anxiety can be caused by the use and abuse of stimulant drugs, including caffeine, over-the-counter wake-up or diet pills, cocaine, and amphetamines.

Chronic use of, as well as withdrawal from, sedative/hypnotic drugs, including alcohol, can precipitate anxiety reactions.

Finally, anxiety can be a psychiatric syndrome defined by the American Psychiatric Association (1980). This category is discussed in detail in chapter 6.

One difficulty is that patients often describe any sense of dysphoria as anxiety. A careful history must be taken to define the precise problems the individual is experiencing, as well as to evaluate the presence of contributing situations such as alcohol and other drug use.

The following case from my chemical dependency treatment program might be instructive. One woman was given diazepam (Valium) when her husband abruptly left her for another woman. Her dose of diazepam escalated over the years as her life became more unmanageable. She continued to deteriorate and had difficulties with her two children and with maintaining employment. She was then placed on an antidepressant along with the diazepam. Tranxene was added, and she was hospitalized. She finally entered treatment for withdrawal from multiple drugs fifteen years after her husband left her. During those fifteen years, she had never received psychotherapy.

Psychotherapy and slow drug withdrawal revealed that the woman had never dealt with the abandonment by her husband. She had had a very disturbed childhood marked by extreme forms of abandonment. Valium was not going to bring her husband back, nor would it help heal the wounds of her childhood traumas.

Insomnia

Insomnia denotes varying degrees of difficulty falling asleep, difficulty staying asleep, and early final awakening. A national survey of physicians revealed a high incidence of insomnia in the population. Seventeen percent of all medical patients and 32 percent of all psychiatric patients complain of insomnia (Kales et al. 1982).

Insomnia is typically a symptom of other difficulties, which include the following:

- Situational problems, such as stress and other environmental difficulties

- Medical problems, such as pain or physical discomfort

- Aging, characterized by nocturnal disturbances after age fifty, often resulting from the fact that people usually get more sleep per twenty-four hours because of naps

- Pharmacological causes resulting from the use of caffeine, alcohol, steroids, or bronchodilators; from drug withdrawal; or from rebound insomnia

- Psychological problems, such as depressive illness and bipolar affective disorder. In addition 70 to 75 percent of any given psychiatric population has some disordered sleep

When a clinician is attempting to treat insomnia, it is important to take a pharmacological history, especially in this drug using society. Caffeine can make it difficult for an individual to fall asleep, while alcohol use can make it difficult for the individual to stay asleep. Tranquilizers, anxiolytics, and other sedative/hypnotics lose their efficacy within one to two weeks and can then cause rebound insomnia.

A proper sleep history includes questions about types of insomnia; nature of the onset; duration; severity and frequency; life situation, including exercise, food intake, and excessive sugar intake; and sleep patterns on a twenty-four-hour basis. Depression, suicidal ideations, and more serious psychopathology must be ruled out. It is believed that most chronic insomnia is due to psychological factors.

There are many approaches to the treatment of insomnia, including the following:

- Behavioral therapy (hypnosis, muscle relaxation, systematic desensitization, and biofeedback)

- Education, which decreases clients' anxiety by letting them know there are no serious consequences associated with partial sleep loss

- Discontinuation of all stimulating substances, including cessation of alcohol and other sedative/hypnotics

- Psychodynamic psychotherapy, which greatly improves the prognosis of chronic insomnia and is more beneficial than behavioral interventions

Pharmacotherapy for insomnia should be limited to those individuals whose symptoms are so severe that they create a functional impairment. The sedative/hypnotics should be used only for short periods of time and in combination with psychotherapy and other nondrug techniques. All clients must first be fully evaluated for chemical dependency (Kales et al. 1982; Kales and Kales 1984).

Many physicians do not heed these cautions. For instance, one of my clients approached her physician for tranquilizers because she was experiencing insomnia due to nervousness about a modeling interview scheduled for the next day. The doctor prescribed flurazepam (Dalmane). The patient remained on that medication for a few months, after which she returned to the physician and complained that the drug was no longer working. He then added diazepam (Valium), to be taken during the day, and increased her nightly dose of flurazepam. In a few months, she returned again, and the doctor switched her from diazepam to alprazolam (Xanax). After two years of this, the patient entered drug treatment. She admitted that prior to using the prescription drugs, she had been dependent on cocaine and alcohol. In fact, her increasing use of and dependency on cocaine was the cause of her insomnia. She had continued to progress in her use of both cocaine and alcohol while she escalated her use of sedative/hypnotics with the doctor's knowledge.

This scenario is all too common. Even if the woman were not chemically dependent, we must ask whether it was appropriate for the physician to prescribe tranquilizers for the woman's insomnia over a modeling interview. Even if we conclude that it was appropriate for the physician to prescribe a sedative/hypnotic, we must question whether it was appropriate for him to continue to prescribe for two years. This physician did not think out the diagnosis, the treatment plan, and the expected therapeutic end points. Failure to establish therapeutic end points and failure to monitor the patient's progress are two mistakes commonly made by physicians who keep patients on these medications for years.

Conclusion

Benzodiazepines do represent an advancement over bromides, barbiturates, and carbamates, but they are clearly overused in both frequency and duration. There is good evidence that the efficacy reported by patients who use them for long periods of time is due to the fact that these patients are chemically dependent and cannot stop the drug abruptly. When they try to get off the drug, they experience increased insomnia and anxiety (withdrawal). When they take another pill, they find that the insomnia and anxiety are relieved. They are unknowingly treating their physical dependency on the drug, not an underlying disease.

Besides creating large cadres of chemically dependent individuals, long-term use of the benzodiazepines without psychotherapy does little to ameliorate patients' underlying difficulties. As Greenblatt et al. (1983) conclude in their extensive review of benzodiazepines, "Since benzodiazepines cure neither anxiety nor insomnia, symptom recurrence can be anticipated after discontinuation of the drug" (p. 357).

Physicians' love affair with benzodiazepines has caused them to move from one drug in this class to the next, newer one. When information about the risks involved in diazepam (Valium) use finally reached the medical profession, physicians switched to prescribing clorazepate (Tranxene), lorazepam (Ativan), and oxazepam (Serax). Currently, alprazolam (Xanax) is enjoying its moment in the sun.

Detoxification centers in chemical dependency treatment programs are often the first to see the untoward effects of overzealous prescribing of these drugs. For instance, the last one hundred women detoxified at our center were dependent on Xanax. It can be predicted that Xanax will become even more of a problem before physicians understand that this drug shares the same limitations as the other benzodiazepines.

Sedation, impaired cognition, tolerance and cross-tolerance, physical dependency, potentiation with other central nervous system depressants, and a withdrawal syndrome are inherent in the use of all benzodiazepines. In addition, the source of the patients' symptoms go untreated for years while they are given these drugs.

Benzodiazepines have their benefits and their risks and are best used in the hands of clinicians who are respectful of their limitations. But "[t]he use of an anxiolytic should not take the place of psychotherapeutic efforts to get at the underlying causes or to provide means of coping with or dissipating anxiety" (Swonger and Constantine 1983, 282). Successfully withdrawing individuals from benzodiazepines involves slow detoxification, treatment for alcoholism and other drug dependencies when they are present, and an aggressive treatment plan aimed at the underlying sources of the complaints.

6

Common Coexisting Disorders in Chemically Dependent Women

Agoraphobia, Eating Disorders, and Depression

Clinicians in the field of alcoholism and other drug dependencies are realizing that while chemical dependency exists alone in some individuals, in other individuals, it might coexist with another mental disorder. Three disorders that affect women more than men are associated with chemical dependency. These are agoraphobia, eating disorders, and depression. All are associated with chemical dependency and can be complicated by physicians misprescribing psychoactive drugs.

The concept of dual diagnosis can be extremely controversial for individuals working in the field of chemical dependency. The controversy originates with the classical way in which alcoholism and other drug dependencies were perceived and treated by the fields of psychiatry and psychology. It was believed that chemical dependency was a symptom of other underlying problems and that once the underlying issues were resolved, the individual would stop using drugs. Many recovering alcoholics talk about spending long hours on the psychiatrist's couch wallowing in their sadness and building up a greater catalog of excuses to drink. This was the "if you had my problems, you'd drink too" era. Clearly, this approach did not work. It failed to recognize that chemical dependency was a disease in and of itself and that the individual could not "get better" until and unless she or he became abstinent and sober.

The controversy also is fueled by physicians who have erroneously diagnosed chemically dependent persons as suffering primarily from depression, anxiety, or insomnia and have then prescribed sedative/hypnotics or tranquilizers. Many doctors fail to understand that chemical dependency in and of itself makes people depressed and anxious and disrupts sleep, and many aid the addiction by supplying more drugs to drug dependent patients.

Most chemical dependency workers realize that an individual must be sober from alcohol and abstinent from all mood-altering drugs in order to begin the process of recovery from the substance use disorder. The problems that were caused by the drugs begin to lift as the individual moves farther along in recovery. Recovering individuals and workers in the field of chemical dependency have had to protect the concept of sobriety and abstinence from outside attacks by groups who believe that alcoholics can learn to drink socially and by physicians who believe that alcoholics can be treated with the right tranquilizer.

With this background it is no wonder that discussions of dual diagnosis are often controversial and difficult. In reality, however, some individuals with substance use disorders do suffer from co-existing mental disorders. Unfortunately, the clients are not helped unless accurate diagnoses are made. If programs and therapists fail to understand that some individuals may indeed be suffering from more than one disorder, they will miss the diagnosis and not be able to treat the client effectively. This becomes particularly important in the treatment of women, who are at a greater risk of experiencing certain types of treatable mental disorders in combination with substance use disorders.

In discussing dual diagnoses, the terms primary and secondary disorders can add to the confusion because they have multiple meanings. *Primary disorder* can mean the disorder that occurred or appeared first, or it can mean the more important of the two disorders and the one that caused the secondary problem. For this discussion, we will use the term primary disorder to mean the disorder that appeared first.

Assessment of Chemical Dependency
in Dual Diagnosis

In most cases of dual diagnosis, the substance use disorder is not caused by the other disorder; rather, the substance use disorder and the other mental disorder coexist side by side. Both problems deserve full and separate evaluation and their own precise and effective treatment plans.

Depression and other problems directly caused by alcoholism and other drug dependencies create a situation in which it is difficult to make a diagnosis of a coexisting disorder. This is particularly true if the chemical dependency preceded the development of the second disorder. It is imperative that the individual be detoxified, clean, and sober before the clinician attempts to assess the presence of a second disorder.

While a person is actively drinking or using other drugs, she should not be given psychoactive medication. In addition, psychological testing is extremely inconclusive at this time, since many drug dependent individuals test depressed while actively using drugs.

During detoxification, it is expected that people will be depressed and/or anxious and will suffer from sleep disturbances and dysphoria. Again, testing during this period is not conclusive.

During the active stage of recovery—approximately three months after detoxification—psychological evaluation and testing are more accurate. At this time, it is easier to evaluate the client for a dual diagnosis, since some of the acute effects of both the drug intoxication and the drug withdrawal will have worn off. No matter what the second diagnosis, abstinence and sobriety are always the treatment for substance use disorders.

Agoraphobia

Agoraphobia falls under the category of anxiety disorders, specifically, phobic disorders. The diagnostic criteria for agoraphobia include the following three definitions:

A. The individual has marked fear of and thus avoids being alone or in public places from which escape might be difficult or help not available in case of sudden incapacitation, e.g., crowds, tunnels, bridges, public transportation.

B. There is increasing constriction of normal activities until the fears or avoidance behavior dominate the individual's life.

C. Not due to a major depressive episode, obsessive compulsive disorder, paranoid personality disorder, or schizophrenia. (American Psychiatric Association 1980, 227)

The demographics for this disease are as follows: 5 percent of the population is affected; 80 percent of those affected are women; onset occurs in the late teens and twenties; and 20 percent of those affected are chemically dependent.

It is now believed that genetics influence the development of this disease. The following findings by Sheehan (1983) support this hypothesis:

1. Those who have close relatives who have (or had) the disease are more likely to develop it than those who do not.

2. The closer the biological relationship to the affected person, the greater the likelihood of developing the disease. This is clear from studies of identical twins.

There is also mounting evidence to support the hypothesis that agoraphobia has a biochemical basis. Sheehan (1983) reports the following evidence:

1. Overexercising has been known to bring on the spells.

2. Infusing sodium lactate into people who had anxiety disease precipitated spells.

3. The locus coeruleus has the highest concentration of norepinephrine.

4. Stimulating the locus coeruleus in monkeys brought on paniclike reactions.

5. The combination of nerve endings overfiring and deficient

inhibition of neurotransmission is believed to form the basis of the panic attack.

6. At a rate of two to four times a week, patients have a sudden discharge of anxiety attacks.

Seven Stages of the Disease

Seven stages of the disease have been outlined by Sheehan (1983).

Spells. Short spells of symptoms occur without warning for no apparent reason. Symptoms can include lightheadedness, fainting, dizzy spells, imbalance, difficulty breathing, palpitations, chest pain or pressure, a choking sensation, paresthesias, hot flashes, nausea, diarrhea, headaches, and derealization and depersonalization.

Panic. Panic is defined as the "mental terror that accompanies the somatic sensations of the body out of control" (Sheehan 1983, 39).

Hypochondriasis. When the patient starts to experience the physical symptoms described under spells, she seeks out medical care to diagnose the etiology of these complaints and to find appropriate treatment. She may go to a gastroenterologist for her gastrointestinal symptoms, a cardiologist for the heart palpitations, or a neurologist for some of the other sensations. These doctors often perform expensive batteries of tests and, when the tests fail to reveal an obvious problem, tell the patient that there is nothing wrong with her. While the physicians might be relieved to find that the patient is not suffering from a "medical" problem, the patient is frustrated that no one has been able to diagnose the source of her very real discomfort.

To date there is no test that will confirm the diagnosis of agoraphobia. A diagnosis can be made on history, but physicians and other clinicians must suspect this diagnosis in order to make it.

Limited Phobias. Agoraphobics experience two to four spontaneous attacks a week. Not understanding that these attacks arise from an internal biochemical imbalance, a woman might associate the attack with what happened at the time of the attack. For example, the woman might have been shopping when the attack came on; to attempt to control the attacks, she avoids shopping. If an attack comes on while she is dining out, she must avoid restaurants, too.

Social Phobias. The individual begins to avoid situations she perceives as stressful in an attempt to control the occurrence of the attacks.

Agoraphobia. The individual's world becomes more and more restricted. At this stage she is involved in extensive phobic avoidance. The word *agoraphobia* comes from the Greek and means, literally, "fear of the marketplace."

Depression. Ultimately the woman develops a sense of hopelessness, helplessness, and worthlessness. At this stage, the woman has no life to speak of and is bound to her home or even to one room in her home.

Agoraphobia and Chemical Dependency

To bolster themselves to go out or to engage in stressful encounters, agoraphobic women often turn to alcohol. Frequently, in their rounds of physicians, they are given tranquilizers and sedative/hypnotics. Typically the alcohol and drugs work for a short time, but increasing doses are needed to get the same effect. Over time, these women become chemically dependent but are still suffering from agoraphobia. They are often referred for chemical dependency treatment or detoxification without the agoraphobia having been diagnosed or properly treated.

Many physicians are placing agoraphobic women on Xanax without first withdrawing them from alcohol and other sedative/hypnotic drugs. It is common for agoraphobics to be dependent on multiple drugs: Xanax, Halcion, Tranxene, and alcohol. Their problems are exacerbated by the fact that they are taking short-acting drugs and then placing themselves, unknowingly, in withdrawal over and over again. Thus they are unwittingly precipitating their own anxiety symptoms (see chapter 5).

While most of the material in Sheehan's book is excellent, his information about the use of Xanax (alprazolam) is dated. His book was published in 1983 and most likely written in 1982. At that time, Xanax was being touted as a drug that would be very useful in the treatment of agoraphobia. Time has shown that, like other benzodiazepines, Xanax initially gives the agoraphobic some relief from the attacks, but the attacks continue to increase over time. In addition, the relief from attacks is not as complete as with the more traditional tricyclic antidepressants or monoamine oxidase (MAO) inhibitors.

Treating Agoraphobia with Antidepressants

Although the average age of onset for agoraphobia is the midtwenties, the average agoraphobic client is between forty and sixty years old. Many agoraphobics have experienced thirty or so years of debilitating attacks and constricted living because the disease so often goes unappreciated and undiagnosed by the medical profession. After years of constricted living, these women not only need the attacks to stop, but also need to learn how to live normal lives.

Antidepressant drugs have been found to be very effective in diminishing both the frequency and intensity of the attacks, but antidepressants alone cannot heal the wounds these women have endured. They need in-depth therapy. As more is known about this disease, we can hope that diagnosis will be made earlier and treatment initiated prior to the development of the severe avoidance behavior.

The antidepressants fall into the following categories:

- Tricyclic antidepressants—imipramine (Tofranil), desipramine (Norpramin), and maprotiline (Ludiomil)

- MAO inhibitors—phenelzine (Nardil), isocarboxazid (Marplan), and tranylcypromine (Parnate)

- Triazolopyridine—trazodone (Desyrel)

Two new drugs also should be mentioned. *Buspirone* is a nonbenzodiazepam anxiolytic that is believed to cause less sedation than Valium-type drugs and supposedly has a low abuse potential. If this drug is as good as it is advertised to be, it might be an effective alternative to benzodiazepines. It must be kept in mind, however, that new drugs often appear better in print than they are in reality. *Burpropione* (Wellbutrin) is a new antidepressant. Because it increases the seizure threshold, however, it is used only if other antidepressants fail to work.

Initiating Antidepressant Therapy

Prior to initiating antidepressant therapy, patients should be alcohol-free. Some physicians believe that tranquilizers and sedative/hypnotics can be abruptly discontinued when antidepressants are initiated, but this can be extremely dangerous. Patients who have been maintained on chronic low doses of these drugs or acute high doses will experience a sedative/hypnotic withdrawal when the drugs are stopped. Increased anxiety, agitation, insomnia, headaches, muscle twitching, and panic attacks are all part of the withdrawal syndrome. The drugs need to be withdrawn slowly and cautiously while the antidepressant therapy is initiated (see chapter 5).

Antidepressants are difficult drugs to initiate. Patients typically experience uncomfortable side effects for approximately two weeks before beginning to feel the positive effects of the medication. The side effects and length of time prior to the onset of the antidepressant effects vary from drug to drug. It is imperative that a physician who is familiar with these medications and familiar with agoraphobia be consulted.

Too often, family physicians who do not have in-depth experience with these medications attempt to initiate antidepressant therapy. The results are dismal. One agoraphobic woman in my practice had been treated first with psychotherapy and then with a tranquilizer by her family physician. After a year without any decrease in her attacks, her family physician initiated the antidepressant imipramine. This would have been a good choice of medication, but the doctor failed to explain the side effects to her. The patient felt extremely uncomfortable, dizzy, groggy, and out of control;

she did not know that these side effects would pass. Unfortunately, the physician's lack of experience with these drugs led him to lower the dose in an attempt to avoid the unavoidable side effects, and the effective dose level was never reached.

Agoraphobic women need a tremendous amount of support during the first month of antidepressant therapy. The following guidelines should be followed when initiating such therapy:

1. Recommend a physician who is well versed in the use of antidepressants.

2. The selection of the antidepressant should be based on a thorough medical history and physical exam.

3. The patient should be given as much detail as possible regarding the side effects and what she can expect. Many physicians withhold this information, believing that the power of suggestion is so strong that the woman will experience the side effects just because she has been warned about them. These physicians underestimate the strength of these drugs and the predictability of the drug response.

4. The patient should be told that her body will become tolerant to most of the side effects and that the positive benefits will be felt in about two to three weeks. Patients need constant reminders that the discomforts they are experiencing will pass.

5. The physician should see the patient twice weekly and be available by phone to help her through this difficult adjustment.

6. The patient should discontinue the use of all products with caffeine, including tea, chocolate, and cola beverages. Any and all chemical stimulants should be avoided.

While this might sound overwhelming for counselors not accustomed to seeing clients on antidepressants, the drugs are extremely beneficial in the treatment of agoraphobia. Once the client begins to feel the effects of medication, she will note a decrease in both the frequency and intensity of attacks. Ultimately she may experience no attacks at all. She will slowly be able to reshape a life that has been marred by a great deal of pain and suffering.

Eating Disorders

The field of chemical dependency is only now beginning to develop a unified philosophy with regard to the etiology and treatment of addictive diseases. While work in the area of eating disorders will benefit from work already done in psychiatry, psychology, addictionology, and sociology, confusion still reigns. The behaviors that are grouped together under the loosely defined heading of eating disorders are in fact extremely varied and may ultimately be found to be distinct and separate entities. The following problems all fall into this category:

- Societal attitudes and norms regarding women and body image (Normal eating is sometimes mislabeled as overeating because society has unrealistic images of what women should look like and because women measure themselves against these norms.)

- Normal overeating

- Compulsive overeating

- Pathological eating disorders (anorexia and bulimia) (American Psychiatric Association 1987, 65)

Societal Attitudes

Of 33,000 American women polled, 80 percent felt the need to be slim in order to be attractive; 41 percent were unhappy with their bodies despite the fact that most were below standard normal weight; and 33 percent relied on laxatives, diuretics, or vomiting for weight control (Boskind-White and White 1986). Another study revealed that 80 percent of ten-year-old girls have already been on a diet and that 5 to 25 percent of those who become anorexic will die (Boskin-White and White 1986). These statistics are overwhelming.

While being overweight is equated with being unhealthy, the truth is that people need to be 20 percent overweight before their weight really becomes a health hazard. Alternatively, individuals will become unhealthy at 15 percent below their ideal weight. Clearly, there is a societal attitude that adversely affects women's body image and holds out an ideal unobtainable by most women except through starvation and strenuous workout schedules. If the norms of society are making individuals sick, we need to ask whether the individuals should be treated or the norms changed.

Normal Overeating

In the course of one month, it is normal for individuals to overeat four times. This overeating should not be considered pathological and does not need treatment.

Compulsive Overeating

Compulsive overeating is not considered a diagnostic category and is not rigidly defined; it is not found under "Eating Disorders" in the DSM IIIR. A compulsive overeater might be roughly defined as someone who eats when not hungry, past the point of normal satiation, to satisfy emotional needs. Neuman and Halvorson (1983) suggest certain questions that can be used to determine whether such an individual needs treatment.

Is the Behavior Compulsive, or is Real Satisfaction Present? In other words, is the individual truly enjoying her food? Is she eating because she enjoys the sensation, or is she eating because she is driven to eat? Everyone overeats on occasion, but they enjoy the smell, tastes, and textures of the food. This kind of overeating differs markedly from a compulsion to overeat, which is devoid of enjoyment, satiation, and satisfaction.

Does the Behavior Have Negative Consequences, such as Illness, Isolation, or Financial Problems? In the absence of true negative consequences, the overeating might not be pathological.

Can the Behavior be Varied, or is there any Flexibility Present?
Does the woman have to overeat every night? If other things come
up, such as an unexpected visit from friends or an invitation to the
movies, can the woman forgo her plans to overeat? More flexibility
represents a healthier situation.

Can the Behavior be Eliminated without Causing Panic? Some individuals can go for long periods of time without overeating. The
ability to stop the overeating behavior without precipitating a panic
might indicate that the overeating is not the expression of a more
deeply rooted problem.

Basically, these questions are similar to the questions chemical
dependency specialists ask to discern whether someone's drug use
is normal or is chronic, compulsive, and out of control. These specialists also are attempting to uncover whether there are any adverse consequences of the drug use and whether the individual
continues to use the drug(s) in the face of these adverse consequences. In evaluating overeating, we must look at the same factors.

Pathological Eating Disorders

Pathological eating disorders is a broad diagnostic term that en-
compasses any dysfunctional behavior marked by a pathological
relationship to food. Anorexia and bulimia fall into this category
and are serious disorders that almost always involve social, sexual,
vocational, and interpersonal dysfunctions. Depression, anxiety,
suicidal ideation, and medical complications frequently appear as
well and must be diagnosed during the initial treatment in order to
design appropriate interventions. Bulimia will be discussed in detail
because of its connection with chemical dependency.

Bulimia is a Greek term that literally means "great hunger."
Clients with this disease, which primarily affects women, are locked
into a cyclical eating pattern. They experience an inordinate desire
for food and then, in an eating binge, consume vast quantities of
food. This binge is followed by a purge, using one or more of these
techniques: vomiting, fasting, constant dieting, or taking laxatives
and/or diuretics.

Diagnostic Criteria for Bulimia. The diagnostic criteria for bulimia include the following:

A. Recurrent episodes of binge eating (rapid consumption of a large amount of food in a discrete period of time, usually less than two hours).
B. At least three of the following:
   1. Consumption of high-caloric, easily ingested food during a binge.
   2. Inconspicuous eating during a binge.
   3. Termination of such eating episodes by abdominal pain, sleep, social interruption, or self-induced vomiting.
   4. Repeated attempts to lose weight by severely restrictive diets, self-induced vomiting, or use of cathartics or diuretics.
   5. Frequent weight fluctuations greater than ten pounds due to alternating binges and fasts.
C. Awareness that the eating pattern is abnormal and fear of not being able to stop eating voluntarily.
D. Depressed mood and self-deprecating thoughts following eating binges.
E. The bulimic episodes are not due to Anorexia Nervosa or any known physical disorder. (American Psychiatric Association 1980, 71)

Characteristics of the Bulimic Client. Bulimics often present with histories of multiple substance abuse disorders. Various other impulse-dominated behaviors also are associated with bulimia. These include shoplifting, promiscuity, and self-mutilation. The following characteristics are often displayed by the bulimic client (Boskind-White and White 1983):

- Distorted body image
- Intelligence, talent, and competence
- Perfectionism
- Obsessive concern with food
- Obsessive concern with body proportions
- Typically normal weight
- Isolationism
- Low self-esteem
- Strong commitment to please others

We can better understand the apparently contradictory behavior of the bulimic if we realize that she recognizes and is driven by two separate, conflicting voices within her. One of these is hypercritical and demands perfection, while the other is rebellious, and impulsive and advocates extremes of indulgence (Garner and Garfinkel 1985).

Bulimia is similar to an addiction in many ways. The bulimic's world is organized around food much the same way a heroin addict's life is organized around drugs. Much time is spent binging and purging, having obsessive ruminations about food, hoarding food, supporting the habit, and concealing the habit. Even the binge–purge cycle (figure 6–1) resembles a drug binge.

Figure 6–1. *The Binge–Purge Cycle*

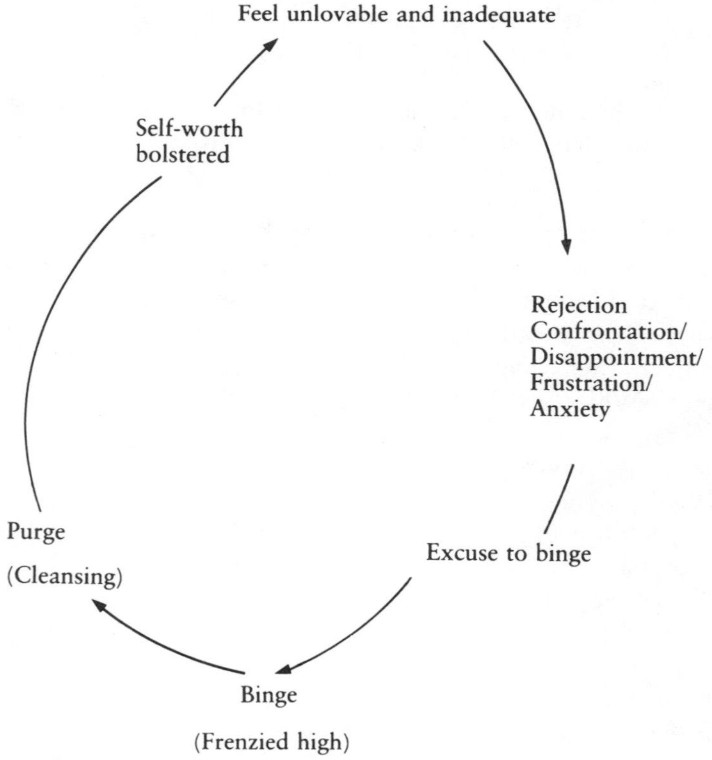

According to Boskind-White and White 1983, the payoffs for binging and purging include a transient release, a frenzied high, a relaxed state, a tranquilizer/antidepressant effect, feelings of uniqueness, a purification rite, a sense of overcoming self-loathing by gaining control, and a transitory sense of self-worth. The tranquilizer effect is seen especially in patients who use massive quantities of laxatives. Laxatives are, in fact, the least effective way to lose calories or weight. What the patient loses is vast quantities of fluids and electrolytes. These women often talk about being so out of it after taking laxatives that they are not able to walk and must sleep.

Drug taking is often associated with bulimia. Large quantities of beer were consumed by one client to facilitate regurgitation. Another client used cocaine to help suppress her appetite and increase her energy. Yet another used intravenous heroin because it caused her to lose weight and suppressed her appetite. The bulimic also chooses to avoid intimacy, difficult situations, or uncomfortable thoughts by binging and purging and/or by using drugs.

Bulimia and Depression. Depressive symptoms are frequently associated with bulimia. According to Garner and Garfinkel 1985, these include depressive thoughts (70 percent), difficulty in concentrating (60 percent), and a depressed mood (lassitude) (52 percent). Some clinicians believe that careful history taking will reveal that the eating disorder preceded the mood disturbance and that there is a coexisting affective disorder (depression) in only a minority of patients (Garner and Garfinkel 1985). Others believe that there is a relationship between primary affective disorders and bulimia (Garner and Garfinkel 1985).

Unlike agoraphobia, bulimia warrants treatment with antidepressants only if there is a coexisting depressive disorder. Antidepressant treatment without therapy has not proven beneficial in the long run for bulimics. The medication often assists in lessening the depression, but the eating disorder will continue unless the patient also receives therapy.

Overeaters Anonymous

Overeaters Anonymous (OA) was developed for people who experience difficulties with chronic overeating without other symptomatology. It was not developed to treat bulimia or anorexia nervosa. While the definitions of chronic overeating and bulimia have merged in the public mind, the reality is that these are very separate and distinct entities. Counselors must learn to distinguish between chronic overeating and bulimia. Sending a bulimic to OA might only reinforce her rigidity and perfectionist thinking. The complexity of bulimia and the deep wounds bulimics have experienced demand the attention of therapists trained in the area of eating disorders.

Considering the similarities between chronic overeating and chemical dependency, it is understandable that the founders of OA would develop a twelve-step program to deal with this problem. Certainly, the cycle of bulimic overeating includes addictive qualities. Its chronic nature, predictability, compulsivity, and sedative effects, along with the increasing isolation it causes, all mimic chemical dependency. Reaching the conclusion from these similarities that a twelve-step program is the best form of treatment overlooks some important issues, however.

On the most superficial level, abstinence from food is not an achievable goal and causes much confusion in people who already suffer from extremely rigid thinking. It is analogous to asking an alcoholic to sit down at a table with alcohol three times a day and "just drink a little." Furthermore, new research shows a strong correlation not only between bulimia and chemical dependency but also between bulimia and depression, shoplifting, promiscuity, and self-mutilation. This suggests that other psychological factors are involved (Garfinkel and Kaplan 1986).

Abstinence in OA means a commitment to a certain eating plan developed with the help of an eating sponsor. One problem is that OA is a young organization, and few of its members have a long history of normal eating patterns. Because of this, a *slip* might become rigidly defined as eating anything that is not on the plan. Thus individuals are constantly slipping and having to start at the beginning with a new "birthday."

For women who are truly suffering from an eating disorder, OA and abstinence serve to reinforce the worst part of the pathology: rigid thinking. OA typically does not have a process for helping people develop a more moderate approach to their own self-regulation and self-judgment. For that reason, OA might be most beneficial for compulsive overeaters who are in need of behavioral and social supports. OA is not sufficient, however, to intervene in the more pathological issues.

> There is a strong tendency for eating disorder patients to engage in dichotomous reasoning (all or none thinking): "If I'm not in complete control, I lose all control. If I gain one pound, I'll go on and gain a hundred pounds. If I eat one cookie, I have ruined the entire day, so I might as well go on and eat more." From these examples, it is apparent that an abstinence goal may encourage more dichotomous reasoning, leading to greater likelihood of failure experiences. These will tend to reduce self-esteem, especially when they attribute their failures to their own personal shortcomings. . . . It appears that abstinence based models may be too simplistic and ineffective, and may even be counterproductive in the treatment of eating disorders. (Rybicki 1986)

Patients need to learn self-control rather than abstinence. Dyadic (all or nothing) thinking must be eliminated, not encouraged.

Specialists in the field of eating disorders agree that a multifaceted treatment approach is essential. Effective treatment might include insight-oriented psychotherapy, supportive therapy, and cognitive behavioral approaches. Individual, group, and family interventions all might be employed at appropriate times in the treatment plan. Clearly, "seasoned therapists agree that singular treatment approaches are ineffective, and may even harm the patient, causing a greater sense of helplessness and failure" (Rybicki 1986).

Depression

There is often confusion about the diagnosis of depression because this word is used to describe many different affective states. Acute dysphoria might be a reaction to physical illness, external life events, certain medications, and ingestion of alcohol or other drugs. Depression is classified as a mood disorder in the revised third edition of the *Diagnostic and Statistical Manual of Mental Disor-*

ders, whereas it is classified as an affected disorder in the original third edition. "Mood refers to prolonged emotion that colors the whole psychic life" (American Psychiatric Association 1987, 224), and the diagnosis of depression as a mood disorder is based on the chronicity of the symptoms.

Depression occurs more frequently in women, whereas bipolar (manic depression) disorder appears to be equally common in males and females (American Psychiatric Association 1987).

Depressive symptoms might include disturbances in all aspects of a person's life, as seen in the following:

- Loss of interest or pleasure
- Not caring anymore
- Withdrawal from family and friends
- Neglect of avocations
- Disturbances in sleep (insomnia or hypersomnia)
- Psychomotor agitation or retardation
- Fatigue, decrease in energy level
- Sense of worthlessness
- Sense of hopelessness and helplessness
- Thoughts of death
- Suicidal ideations

An untreated episode will last six months or longer, usually followed by a remission. If some symptoms last longer, this is considered chronic depression (American Psychiatric Association 1987). Demographics of this disorder are as follows:

- Range for females: 9 to 26 percent of the population

- Range for males: 5 to 12 percent of the population

- Twice as common in females as in males

- 1.5 to 3 times more common among first degree biologic relatives with the disorder than among the general public (American Psychiatric Association 1987)

- Age of onset: average age late twenties but can begin at any age, including infancy (American Psychiatric Association 1987)

International comparisons of diagnosed and treated cases are consistent with the outcome of community surveys. Weissman and Klerman (1982) report that "[w]omen preponderate in the rates of depression" (p. 100) and postulate four possible etiologies for this pattern:

1. The possibility that trends are spurious because of artifacts produced by methods of reporting symptoms, or that they are real because of;
2. Biological susceptibility: possibly genetic or female endocrine;
3. Psychosocial factors such as social discrimination; or
4. Female learned helplessness. (p. 95)

The authors conclude that "[m]any more women than men are depressed in Western society and none of the above stated areas will solely account for the preponderance" (p. 95).

Focusing on psychosocial factors and female learned helplessness, it is important to point out that women who subscribe to traditional female roles are at a higher risk for developing depression than are women who demonstrate more malelike or androgenous traits (Bem 1974; Tinsley, Sullivan-Guest, and McGuire 1984). Indeed, the distinguishing traits of depression—"vulnerability to loss, inhibition of action and assertion, inhibition of anger, and low self-esteem" (Kaplan 1986, 234)—are all key elements in the development of the female gender identity.

Chemically dependent women have been found to score higher on the feminine side of this scale than non–chemically dependent women. One can begin to understand why chemically dependent women are more prone to major depressive mood disorders when their high femininity scores are coupled with their dysfunctional families of origin, low levels of education, and high rates of unemployment or underemployment. See chapter 1 of this book for a detailed discussion of these factors.

Drugs and Depression

The role of depression in women as an antecedent or a consequence of problem drinking has been explored by Gomberg and Lisansky

1984. It is important to note that "daughters of alcoholics raised in their own families manifested significantly more depression than daughters of alcoholics raised in nonalcoholic families and more than the control adoptive with no history of family alcoholism" (Gomberg and Lisansky 1984, 242). In addition, women whose depression preceded their alcoholism had more severe disease courses, such as increased suicides, and family histories of more female relatives with mood disorders (Gomberg and Lisansky 1984).

A study of the alcohol misuse and depression of women criminals revealed that depressive alcoholic subjects had a greater rate of depression during follow-up than nonalcoholic index depressives. This study concluded that depression within the setting of alcohol dependency was predictive of future depression and suicide attempts (Martin, Cloninger, and Guze 1985).

Case Presentation

Andrea is a forty-six-year-old woman who entered our women's chemical dependency program for treatment of cocaine and alcohol dependency. Her mother gave her amphetamines starting at age eleven to control her weight, and Andrea remained on speed until the past two years, when she replaced the speed with cocaine. Andrea had always used alcohol to balance the speed or cocaine highs. She entered treatment desperately seeking assistance for the drug dependencies and for relief of an overwhelming sense of hopelessness.

Andrea's family history revealed that she came from a wealthy family. She stated: "I was raised to be an adornment for a wealthy successful man, and my brother was raised to be a wealthy successful man." Her mother was preoccupied with Andrea's appearance, to the point of putting her on diets from the time she was two years old. While she felt rejection and constant criticism from her mother, Andrea looked forward to her too infrequent contacts with her loving but busy businessman father. Basically, she stated, she was miserable and felt as if she never fit. Her father died, and Andrea reported living in terror that her mother would die.

Andrea was married once and has two adult children from that relationship. Her husband abruptly left her ten years ago in a divorce that she did not want or support. Adding injury to insult, he recently married a model who is younger than their children.

Financially, Andrea is well off and manages houses that she owns.

A medical evaluation revealed that Andrea was quite hypothyroid (low thyroid). This led to speculation that, in part, she might have been attempting to treat the symptoms of hypothyroidism with speed and then cocaine. She was given thyroid hormone, but six months later was doubling this dose.

Ultimately, Andrea was attending individual therapy, AA, NA, and OA. She was attending three self-help meetings a day and seeing an acupuncturist and chiropractor three times a week. After experiencing a number of slips, she was finally on a good recovery program and maintained sobriety for one year. During this time she appeared to be living a satisfying life.

After another year, Andrea returned to the treatment program sober but experiencing hypersomnia, inability to complete work, a 20-pound weight gain, an overwhelming sense of helplessness, and suicidal ideations that had been present for six weeks. Her depression was palpable, and after a thorough medical and psychological evaluation, the possibility of using psychotherapeutics (antidepressants) was discussed with her.

Andrea voiced concern that she would be ostracized by her AA group and that usage of an antidepressant, even under proper medical supervision, would be viewed as a slip. With Andrea's written permission, her therapist and physician discussed this situation with her AA sponsor. Fortunately, he understood and facilitated AA's acceptance of Andrea's much needed medication. Andrea's depression responded rapidly to the combination of the tricyclics, individual therapy three times weekly, a weekly assessment by her physician, and continued active participation in AA.

This is a classic case in which treatment for chemical dependency was a necessary but insufficient approach to dealing with a person's pain.

Conclusion

To treat chemically dependent individuals effectively, one must know the field of chemical dependency and also realize that some clients will have coexisting disorders. Some of these disorders, such as agoraphobia, bipolar depression (manic depression), and major unipolar depressive disorders may demand intervention with psychoactive drugs such as antidepressants or Lithium. To withhold proper treatment from these clients is as negligent as prescribing tranquilizers for an active alcoholic.

Many chemical dependency workers have assumed a rigidly negative attitude toward all psychoactive drugs. These attitudes can prevent the counselor from diagnosing debilitating, coexisting disorders and may undermine the design of an effective treatment plan. Likewise, preconceived notions about the effectiveness and appropriateness of twelve-step programs may lead counselors to recommend ineffective, frustrating programs that only exacerbate the client's underlying condition. Through continuing education and good clinical case supervision, counselors in the field of chemical dependency can enhance their ability to assess and effectively refer or treat their clients with coexisting disorders.

7

Cocaine: The Perfect Trap for Women

Cocaine may well be seen as the perfect drug for women in the 1980s. Once limited to use by streetwise heroin addicts, cocaine has recently found its way into the mainstream of Middle America. The change in the popular perception of cocaine from a highly illegal to a high-status drug has had a tremendous effect on women. As cocaine has become more acceptable and more available, more women have felt comfortable experimenting with it. Cocaine has been used as a membership card and as a way to make people feel successful.

Cocaine is a particularly seductive and destructive drug for women. This chapter explores the drug in detail—its history, pharmacology, and special effects on women—and offers treatment approaches designed for the woman client.

Manufacture of Cocaine

The manufacture of cocaine is illustrated in figure 7–1. For cocaine to be smoked, it must be converted to the free-base form. "Basing" entails a chemical procedure in which an alkali is added to the cocaine hydrochloride. The cocaine free base is then precipitated by using a solvent, such as ether. This procedure is cumbersome and often ends in a conflagration because of the volatile nature of ether.

It was discovered that the last stage could be eliminated and

Figure 7–1. *The Manufacture of Cocaine*

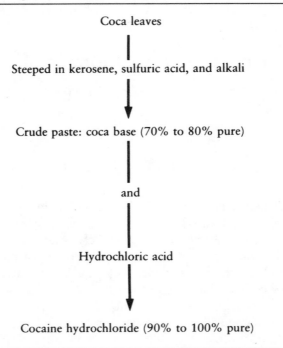

Coca leaves

Steeped in kerosene, sulfuric acid, and alkali

Crude paste: coca base (70% to 80% pure)

and

Hydrochloric acid

Cocaine hydrochloride (90% to 100% pure)

the free base extracted directly from the alkalinized cocaine by evaporating the water. The waxy material produced is best known as crack. This procedure is easier and eliminates the need to use potentially dangerous solvents, allowing dealers to mass-produce large quantities of free-base cocaine at a low cost. Crack is sold in rocklike pieces at very affordable prices. One piece of crack can sell for $5, making it inexpensive enough for even school-age children.

History of Cocaine

It is believed that the cultivation and use of coca started before A.D. 1200. The coca shrubs, *Erythroxylon coca,* are native to the eastern slopes of the Andes. The plant is legal in Peru and Bolivia and has been cultivated by the Indians of South America for thousands of years.

The Incas regarded coca as a divine plant and worshiped it as such. According to an Inca legend, the Children of the Sun presented mankind with coca to "satisfy the hungry, provide the weary and fainting with new vigour, and cause the unhappy to forget their miseries" (Weil 1983).

To extract the cocaine, South American Indians put dried coca leaves in their mouths together with a small amount of alkali in the form of lime or ash. After sucking on the wad for thirty minutes, they swallowed the juice and spat out the residue.

In 1859, cocaine was isolated in its pure form from the coca leaf by a German scientist. In the late 1800s, cocaine was a popular ingredient in both European and American tonics and waters. Coca-Cola began as one of these products.

Many scientists throughout Europe, including Sigmund Freud, expressed unbridled enthusiasm for this drug. After experimenting with cocaine, an Italian neurologist wrote: "God is unjust because he made man incapable of sustaining the effect of coca all life long. I would rather have a life span of 10 years with coca than one of one million centuries without coca." (Weil 1983).

In 1884 Freud personally experimented with cocaine. In his article "On Coca," he praised its value in treating depression, nervousness, morphinism, alcoholism, and other problems. (Byck 1974) Freud treated his own depression with cocaine and found "exhilaration and lasting euphoria, which in no way differs from the euphoria of the healthy person. . . . You perceive an increase in self-control and possess more vitality and capacity for work. . . . In other words, you are simply more normal, and it is soon hard to believe that you are under the influence of any drug" (Byck 1974).

One physician in Europe had become addicted to morphine while treating a painful neuroma that had developed at the site of an amputation. Freud put this man on cocaine to get him off morphine. Later, it was said that he was transformed from "the first morphine addict in Europe to the first cocaine addict in Europe" (Byck 1974). As this physician used increasingly greater quantities of cocaine, he experienced severe psychological deterioration and paranoid hallucinations. By this time, hundreds of cases of psychosis, convulsions, death, and compulsive use were being linked to cocaine.

Three years after his work with cocaine began, Freud was accused of recklessness and irresponsibility in regard to the drug. One addiction expert charged Freud with "unleashing the third scourge of mankind [after alcohol and morphine]" (Jones 1961). One of Freud's patients died of an overdose of cocaine, which Freud had prescribed (Byck 1974). Freud was later to describe this as the darkest and least successful period of his life. (Byck 1974)

By 1887 Freud did admit that cocaine injection produced the adverse effects of mental and physical deterioration, paranoia, and hallucinations. By 1891 four hundred cases of cocaine intoxication and thirteen deaths were reported (Woods and Downs 1973).

By the early 1900s, the public's perception of cocaine had changed dramatically. It was no longer seen as an innocuous drug and "articles in leading newspapers, such as the New York Times, reported that cocaine use resulted in mass murders by crazed Blacks whose marksmanship was greatly improved by the drug" (Smith 1986). This marked change in the perception of cocaine was one of the factors that led to enactment of the Harrison Act of 1914, which criminalized both cocaine and opiate use (Smith 1986).

Cocaine in Mainstream America

Until the late 1970s, cocaine continued to be perceived as a dangerous drug. It was also rather expensive and not widely available. Cocaine made its way into the mainstream through the legal use of amphetamines.

In the 1960s and 1970s, amphetamine (speed) use and abuse became widespread: first through legally prescribed sources, then through illicit diversion of the legal pharmaceutical products, and finally through illegal manufacturing. Speed found its way into Middle America through the prescribing practices of physicians.

When the legal source of amphetamines began to dry up because of tougher laws, an exposed market was ready to make the switch to another upper—cocaine. The fact that cocaine is much shorter acting than most amphetamines (two hours versus twelve hours) and, when snorted, has a more subtle effect than amphetamines might have led to the widespread belief that cocaine is a lightweight or innocuous drug.

Just as amphetamines assisted in the movement of cocaine into Middle America, cocaine may be assisting the introduction of heroin into Middle America. Historically there have been cycles in drug use, moving from uppers to a combination of uppers and downers to downers alone. Many people are now snorting heroin to help come down from cocaine.

As the potency of cocaine increases (for example, with the smoking of crack cocaine), individuals will seek stronger and stronger depressant drugs to offset the stimulating effects of the cocaine. Researchers and clinicians around the country are reporting increased use of heroin, alcohol, sedative/hypnotics, and marijuana by regular cocaine users to counteract the effects of sustained cocaine use (NIDA 1986).

At the same time that more potent forms of cocaine are becoming widely available, more potent heroin is also flooding the market. Reports of the appearance of a dark, gummy form of heroin known as black tar or tootsie roll are increasing. The purity of this heroin is reported to be as high as 85 percent, in contrast to the 2 to 4 percent purity generally found in Mexican brown or Asian heroin (NIDA 1986). It is not difficult to see that snorting cocaine could give way to snorting heroin and that smoking crack could give way to "chasing the dragon," that is, putting heroin on aluminum foil and smoking it.

The crossover from cocaine to heroin also appears to be bringing with it the movement from snorting to IV drug use. Ironically, Middle America, which once eschewed shooting up, is discovering IV drug use just at a time when the threat of AIDS makes sharing needles a potentially lethal practice.

In some areas, the widespread use of cocaine is also reopening the speed craze. Illegal production of methamphetamine has increased, and the reappearance of this particularly potent form of speed does not bode well.

Epidemiology

Cocaine use among women was extremely limited when the drug was closely associated with the underground and viewed as highly illicit. As cocaine use has moved into Middle America, however, it has gained widespread acceptance among women.

The following nationwide statistics (NIDA 1986) demonstrate the dramatic increase in the use of cocaine:

1959   10,000 people had used cocaine within the past 10 months

1979   10 million people had used cocaine

1985   22 million people had used cocaine; 5.8 million were current (past month) users

The increase in cocaine use has been paralleled by the dramatic increase in cocaine-related deaths over the past five years, as is reflected by statistics from the Drug Abuse Warning Network (DAWN) (NIDA 1987):

Year Ending June	Number of Deaths Due to Cocaine
1982	254
1983	470
1984	606
1985	930
1986	1,129

The 800-COCAINE hot line provides the following statistics on women and cocaine (800-Cocaine Hot line 1985):

• The average age is thirty.

• Sixty-five percent are white.

• Almost half earn $25,000 or more per year.

• Forty-seven percent are daily users who use 5.7 grams weekly ($450).

- Two-thirds use other drugs and alcohol to come down from cocaine.

- Twenty percent free-base.

- Thirteen percent use cocaine intravenously.

- Twenty-one percent deal cocaine.

It must be kept in mind that these statistics are based on women who believe they have a problem with cocaine and have called the hot line. They might not reflect the entire population of women who are using cocaine. Despite this caveat, cocaine use has clearly emerged as a leading drug problem among women in this country.

Pharmacology

Cocaine has two distinct pharmacological actions: It is a CNS stimulant and a peripheral anesthetic. Cocaine blocks the reuptake of the catecholamine neurotransmitters norepinephrine and dopamine. Cocaine does not act as a direct neurotransmitter; instead, it enhances the body's own catecholamines. It is believed that this ultimately leads to a depletion of the body's neurotransmitters.

The acute effects of cocaine include CNS stimulation, appetite suppression, increased sexual drive, decreased sensitivity, enhanced sense of competency, and euphoria. Cocaine has been described as the high with the low because there is a rapid shift from ecstasy to misery. Unrestrained enthusiasm is followed by disillusionment, and the user is impelled to use again in order to ward off the dysphoria that follows the use of this drug.

Acute positive effects include feelings of pleasure, euphoria, elation, ecstasy, hyperarousal, hypervigilance, and hyperexcitability. Acute negative effects include anxiety, agitation, nausea, light sensitivity, increased blood pressure, decreased heart rate, increased respiratory rate, paranoia, apathy, confusion, and "snowlights" (spots in eyes).

The postcocaine state includes headache, unhappiness, dysphoria, and lethargy. In an attempt to postpone or ward off the postcocaine depression, cocaine users feel compelled to continue to use more cocaine. If an individual has become wired because of the continuous use of cocaine, she or he might elect to come down from the high using a depressant such as alcohol, heroin, or tranquilizers. The speed effect of the cocaine makes it possible for individuals to drink very large quantities of alcohol without feeling the typically inebriating effects of this drug.

Cocaine Overdose

The following are hallmarks of acute overdose: dysphoric agitation, extreme anxiety, fever, convulsions (seizures), ventricular arrhythmias, and cardiorespiratory collapse. Acute overdose can be life threatening. In 1985 cocaine accounted for the largest number of overdoses nationwide. Overdose treatment includes IV diazepam (Valium) for seizure control, external cooling for hyperthermia, and antiarrhythmic drugs for cardiac arrhythmias.

Chronic high-dose cocaine use produces an increased postsynaptic sensitivity to dopamine. This leads to what has been termed a kindling effect. When the high-dose user abstains from cocaine for a short time and then returns to use, she or he may experience a severe physiological reaction to even low doses of the drug. This can lead to increased toxicity, involving cardiac, psychiatric, or neurological symptoms. It is this kindling effect that might be responsible for some of the recent cocaine overdoses (Smith 1986).

Cocaine Psychosis

Chronic use of cocaine or large acute doses can lead to the development of a toxic psychosis. The hallmarks of cocaine psychosis include tactile hallucinations; "coke bugs"; ulcerations; visual, auditory, and gustatory hallucinations; and paranoia. Individuals might present with excoriations on the arms and legs where they tried to dig out the bugs they felt were crawling under their skin. One of my patients thought she had a bad case of scabies but was in fact experiencing the tactile hallucination that has come to be called "coke bugs."

Paranoia is a common side effect of chronic cocaine use. Individuals have been known to buy guns and lock themselves in a room because of the belief that they were being followed or that someone was out to get them. In a milder form, clients admit that they have to keep looking over their shoulders because they feel someone is watching them.

Cocaine's Reinforcing Properties

One of cocaine's major properties is its ability to make the user want more cocaine. This has been demonstrated in animal studies. All animals will work harder for cocaine than for any other drug. If monkeys are given an unlimited access to cocaine, they will bar-press for this drug until they die of seizures. The monkeys will avoid food, water, and sex while working to get cocaine; in fact, monkeys prefer cocaine to food even if they are starving. Monkeys also prefer a higher dose of cocaine delivered with an electric shock to a lower dose delivered without an electric shock (Johanson et al 1985).

This particular property of cocaine might make it one of the more dangerous drugs available today. While it is believed that chemical dependency is in part genetically and biologically based, cocaine might be one drug that can be extremely dangerous even to individuals who have no family history of chemical dependency. If an individual exposes herself or himself to cocaine often enough, she or he will develop a craving for this drug based only on its pharmacological property of reinforcement.

Women's Complaints and Susceptibility

According to the 800-COCAINE hot line (1985), women have expressed the following complaints related to their chronic use of cocaine: severe depression, irritability, loss of sex drive, suicide attempts, job problems, severe headaches, seizures, and inability to sleep for days on end. Despite these problems, today's expectations for women might make cocaine a particularly appealing drug. In many ways, women are expected to be superwomen, have prepubescent figures, and be sexually available. While ads tell women that they have come a long way, the reality seems quite different. The women's liberation movement of the 1970s may have given women permission to be more like men, but it did little in the way of giving both men and women the permission to be more like women. As a result, women are still burdened with the perceived female responsibility of caring for the children and the home, which they must attempt to juggle with their careers.

As discussed in earlier chapters, society still denigrates things perceived as being feminine or female, and as a result, women in general and chemically dependent women in particular have a lower self-esteem than do men. Growing up female in a society that undervalues and denigrates the role of women also results in high levels of depression and anxiety and in a sense of powerlessness. Learned helplessness acts in concert with depression and low self-esteem to immobilize many women.

Cocaine provides people, for a fleeting moment, with a sense of accomplishment, self-worth, and potency. Many women report that they felt worthwhile for the first time in their life while on cocaine. This fleeting sense of well-being is itself reinforcing. Women will go back to cocaine again and again to try to experience these feelings of control and power.

Body Image

If we keep in mind the fact that many women are introduced to speedlike drugs through legal prescriptions of amphetamines for weight loss, it is not surprising that women believe one of the benefits of cocaine is appetite suppression. The modern standard of feminine beauty is a prepubescent, malelike figure, which is unobtainable by most women except through vigorous exercise and starvation.

Women decry the natural surges of estrogen that direct the specifically feminine distribution of fat to hips, thighs, belly, and breasts. Flagellating themselves with obsessive workout schedules and/or starvation, some women change their fat-to-muscle ratio to the point where they no longer have their menstrual periods (amenorrhea).

Unfortunately, cocaine is perceived as a woman's ally in her struggle to obtain the perfect body. Suppressing appetite and giving a false sense of energy, cocaine is erroneously seen by some women as a useful adjunct to or substitute for a workout schedule.

Sexual Availability

The sexual liberation of the 1960s and 1970s can be seen as giving women permission to engage in a freer, more malelike sexuality. This certainly has had its benefits, but perhaps one of the drawbacks has been a failure to appreciate the real differences in female and male sexuality. Women were given permission to unlock their genitals from their hearts and minds and to engage in sexuality that perhaps had more to do with genital friction than with love. Many women found this mindless, heartless sex to be dystonic with their own values and urges. In an attempt to override their natural inclinations and to conform to a perceived societal expectation, many women used drugs to lubricate the social situation.

One woman in our cocaine group said that it never dawned on her that she could say no to demands for sexual relations on the first date. Others in the group reinforced the belief that women were supposed to be sexually available. It is interesting to note that all the women in the group were aware of not wanting to have intimate sex this quickly in the relationship but felt that it was expected. They all admitted that they used cocaine and alcohol to make their bodies do what their hearts and minds were not quite ready to do. Treatment included giving these women permission to say no. Not using cocaine and alcohol actually made it much easier for the women to respect and not override their natural inclinations.

In addition to making sex a bit easier on first dates, cocaine initially increases a woman's sex drive or libido. Again, by buying into some Hollywood notion of how often a woman should desire sex, many women feel self-critical about their own natural rhythms. Cocaine is perceived as a good way to make a woman feel more sexual if she is not originally in the mood. In the beginning, this can make a woman feel as though she fits the societal norm of a healthy, sexually attractive woman.

Sexual Dysfunction

Although cocaine is highly touted as an aphrodisiac, it is actually very poor at enhancing the sexual response cycle. The one segment of the cycle that is positively affected by cocaine is the sexual drive (what used to be called the libido). While cocaine does increase the sexual drive, it does not enhance sensation or physical sensitivity and may in fact decrease them. This peculiar combination of enhanced sexual drive and decreased sensation is particularly frustrating and can lead to what cocaine users admit is bizarre or aberrant sexual behavior.

Cocaine's effect on sexuality is quite different from that of alcohol, which seems through disinhibition (a release of inhibitions) to give the individual permission to engage in sexual activities that she really wanted to pursue anyway. With cocaine, driven by the combination of highly enhanced sexual drive and a diminution of sensation, individuals might engage in sexual activities that are counter to their true value systems. Such activities might include group sex, anonymous sex, marathon sexual encounters, and compulsive masturbatory behavior.

As with other drugs, the movement from acute intermittent use of cocaine to chronic high-dose use brings with it a decrease in sexual desire. At this point, sexual functioning is severely impaired and the drug becomes a replacement for sexual intimacy. Sexual function also might be impaired because of the route of administration of cocaine. Placed vaginally or rectally, cocaine can cause a drying of the mucous membranes and lead to irritation, discomfort, and painful intercourse (dysparunia).

Cocaine and Dependency on Men

Many women's cocaine habit is maintained by supplies from boyfriends. Thus it is possible for women to become addicted to large quantities of cocaine for long periods of time without suffering the financial consequences. Running out of money or depleting financial resources are end points that can act as levers to force a person to seek treatment. For men, the lack of available financial resources may be the rate limiting factor in the addiction process, but women are often buffered from this. When women are being supported by their male friends, they lose one more potential impetus to stop using and seek treatment.

Cocaine often increases women's dependency on men. Some women are well aware of the fact that they are maintaining relationships solely for the purpose of keeping their cocaine supply lines open. "Cocaine whores" barter their bodies and relationships in exchange for cocaine. This happens at great cost to the women, usually in terms of their independence and sense of self-worth.

One story may be instructive. Mary's cocaine addiction became so intense that she had to snort up every ten minutes to feel right. She could not begin to afford this habit on her waitress's salary, but she found that if she maintained sexual relationships with men who used cocaine, she would always have a ready supply. Ultimately she needed to be with men who dealt cocaine because her habit was so large. In recovery, Mary realized that she had become a prisoner not only of cocaine, but also of the men who supplied her with it. As happens to so many women who become dependent on cocaine, Mary felt much guilt and shame over what she had done while loaded on cocaine and in order to maintain her habit.

Treatment

Because cocaine can be a particularly seductive drug for women, women in treatment must explore the positive effects they experienced from the drug. These women should have the opportunity to discuss what they liked about cocaine, and treatment planning should include developing healthy ways for obtaining what the women wanted from the drug. The loss of cocaine should not mean the loss of feeling good, competent, worthy, attractive, or sexual. Women must learn that it was not wrong to want from life what they wanted from cocaine, but just that cocaine made false promises that it could not keep. Through an active recovery program, treatment can give a woman a sense of hope that she can attain much of the satisfaction and self-esteem she craves without the use of drugs.

Relapse prevention includes abstinence from all drugs. Many cocaine users do not believe that they must lead a life of sobriety and abstinence because they believe that their only problem is with cocaine. They must be taught the disease concept of chemical dependency, the interactivity of all psychoactive drugs, and the fact that use of any psychoactive drug can stimulate a craving for cocaine. As with other forms of chemical dependency, it must be stressed that recovery from cocaine addiction is a lifelong process.

Women in recovery should have access to same-sex groups in which they can work out their feelings about bizarre sexual occurrences, dependency on men, and feelings of guilt and shame. What women did while using cocaine and what women did to maintain their cocaine habits must be fully explored in the context of supportive, empathic all-women groups. This includes exploring the issue of violence. Many women find themselves involved in criminal activities and violence for the first time in their lives while they are dependent on cocaine. Mixed male-female groups are often too threatening to women who are trying to work through these difficult issues.

As noted above, cocaine does not act as a neurotransmitter, but instead depletes the body's own transmitters. Cocaine withdrawal symptoms and drug hunger appear to be related in part to the depletion of dopamine and norepinephrine. The amino acid L-tryptophan is the precursor for dopamine, and the amino acid tyrosine is the precursor for norepinephrine. Therefore, it has been postulated that supplementing these amino acids will assist the individual through the withdrawal period. It must be understood that the efficacy and safety of these regimens have not been scientifically studied but are based on anecdotal reports. The suggested doses are as follows: L-tryptophan—1 gram before breakfast and lunch, 2 to 4 grams at bedtime; tyrosine—1 gram before breakfast and lunch (Smith 1986).

In addition, Vereby and Gold (1984) believe that chronic use of cocaine may lead to the depletion of B-complex and C vitamins.

They suggest that individuals withdrawing from cocaine be treated with these vitamins. Given the fact that chemically dependent individuals have difficulty in using any substance in moderation, their use of vitamins and amino acids should be closely monitored.

Conclusion

When we understand the pressures faced by women in the 1980s, we can better understand why cocaine is a particularly seductive drug for them. To treat cocaine dependent women effectively, programs must understand the unique properties of this potent drug and appreciate the guilt- and shame-provoking incidents these women have experienced because of their use of it.

Successful treatment interventions must include understanding the positive effects women experience through cocaine and designing recovery plans that allow the achievement of some of these goals without the use of drugs. All-women groups are imperative to provide a safe, empathic environment in which women can relate their drug histories and work through their guilt, shame, sense of loss, and dependency on men. Attention to the clients' nutritional needs might help ameliorate some of the fatiguing and depressing effects caused by cocaine's depletion of the neurotransmitters.

References

Chapter 1

Beckman, Linda J., and Hortensia Amaro. 1984. "Patterns of Women's Use of Alcohol Treatment Agencies." In *Alcohol Problems in Women: Antecedents, Consequences and Intervention,* edited by S.C. Wilsnack and L.J. Beckman. New York City: The Guilford Press.

Black, R., and J. Mayer, 1980. "Parents with Special Problems: Alcoholism and Opiate Addictions. In *Child Abuse and Neglect* 4 45–54.

Beschner, G.M., B.G. Reed, and J. Mondanaro, eds. 1981. *Treatment Services for Drug Dependent Women.* Vol. 1. Rockville, Maryland: National Institute on Drug Abuse, DHHS Publ. No. (ADM) 81-1177.

Hill, Shirley Y. 1984. "Vulnerability to the Biomedical Consequences of Alcoholism and Alcohol-Related Problems among Women." In *Alcohol Problems in Women. See* Beckman and Amaro 1984.

Kovach, Judith. 1981. "Developing and Managing Referral Linkages for Drug Dependent Women." In *Treatment Services for Drug Dependent Women.* Vol. 1. *See* Beschner, Reed, and Mondanaro 1981.

Mills, B.B., and M.B. Nelson. 1982. "Perspectives on Treatment of Drug Dependent Lesbians." In *Treatment Services for Drug Dependent Women,* vol. 2, edited by B.G. Reed, G.M. Beschner, and J. Mondanaro. Rockville, Maryland: National Institute on Drug Abuse, DHHS Publ. No. (ADM) 82-1219.

Mondanaro, Josette. 1981. "Medical Services for Drug Dependent Women." In *Treatment Services for Drug Dependent Women.* Vol. 1. *See* Beschner, Reed, and Mondanaro 1981.

Mondanaro, J., et al. 1982. "Sexuality and Intimacy as Barriers to Recovery for Drug Dependent Women." In *Treatment Services for Drug Dependent Women.* Vol. 2. *See* Mills and Nelson 1982.

NASADAD. 1987. *State Response and Services Related to Alcohol and Drug Abuse Problems.* Washington, D.C.: National Association of State Alcohol and Drug Abuse Directors (NASADAD).

Reed, B.G. 1981. "Intervention Strategies for Drug Dependent Women: An Introduction," In *Treatment Services for Drug Dependent Women.* Vol. 1. *See* Beschner, Reed and Mondanaro, 1981.

Reed, B.G. 1985. "Drug Misuse and Dependency in Women: The Meaning and Implications of Being Considered a Special Population or Minority Group." In *The International Journal of the Addictions,* Vol. 20 #1:13–61.

Ryan, V.S. 1980. "Differences Between Males and Females in Drug Treatment Programs." In *Drug Dependence and Alcoholism* edited by A. Schecter. New York: Plenum Press.

Sandelowski, Margarette. 1981. *Women, Health, and Choice.* Englewood Cliffs, New Jersey: Prentice-Hall, Inc.

Soler, Esta G., and Grace Dammann. 1981. *Women in Crisis: Drug Use and Abuse.* Sacramento, California: State of California Department of Alcohol and Drug Programs, ADP–81–4.

Sutker, Patricia B. 1981. "Drug Dependent Women: An Overview of the Literature." In *Treatment Services for Drug Dependent Women.* Vol. 1. *See* Beschner, Reed, and Mondanaro 1981.

Chapter 2

Beletsis, Susan G., and Stephanie Brown. 1981. "A Developmental Framework for Understanding the Adult Children of Alcoholics." *Focus on Women: Journal of Addictions and Health* 2(Winter).

Brown, Stephanie, and Susan, G. Beletsis. 1986. "The Development of Family Transference in Groups for the Adult Children of Alcoholics." *International Journal of Group Psychotherapy* 36(January):97–114.

Cermak, Timmen L., and Stephanie Brown. 1982. "Interactional Group Therapy with the Adult Children of Alcoholics." *International Journal of Group Psychotherapy* 32(July):375–89.

Miller, Alice. 1981. *The Drama of the Gifted Child: How Narcissistic Parents Form and Deform the Emotional Lives of Their Talented Children.* New York: Basic Books, Inc.

———. 1984. *Thou Shalt Not Be Aware.* New York: Farrar-Strauss-Giroux.

Mondanaro, J., et al. 1982. "Sexuality and Fear of Intimacy as Barriers to Recovery for Drug Dependent Women." In *Treatment Services for Drug Dependent Women,* vol. 2, edited by B.G. Reed, G.M. Beschner, and J. Mondanaro. Rockville, Maryland: National Institute on Drug Abuse, DHHS Publ. No. (ADM) 82-1219.

Norwood, Robin. 1985. *Women Who Love Too Much.* New York City: Pocket Books.

Chapter 3

Bean, Xylina. 1986. "Overview of Neonatal Effects in Infants Exposed to PCP, Cocaine and Other Drugs." Paper presented at Update 86: Chemical Dependency and Pregnancy. Tri-County Chemical Dependency and Pregnancy Project, San Francisco, April 25.

———. 1988. Telephone conversation with author, March.

Mondanaro, Josette. 1977. "Women, Pregnancy, Children and Addiction." *Journal of Psychedelic Drugs* 9(January–March):59–68.

NIDA. 1979. *Drug Dependency in Pregnancy: Clinical Management of Mother and Child.* Services Research Monograph Series. Rockville, Maryland: National Institute on Drug Abuse (NIDA).

United States Department of Health and Human Services (DHHS). 1980. *The Health Consequences of Smoking for Women: A Report of the Surgeon General.*

Chapter 4

Ashery, R., ed. 1986. *AIDS and the IV Drug User: A Training Program in Education, Risk Assessment, and Treatment Planning for Drug Abuse Program Counselors (Participants Guide).* Rockville, Maryland: National Institute on Drug Abuse.

Centers for Disease Control. 1985a. "Recommendations for Assisting in the Prevention of Perinatal Transmission of HTLV/LAV and AIDS. *Morbidity and Mortality Weekly Report (MMWR)* 34(December 6):721–32.

———. 1985b. *Safety Precautions for Persons at High Risk for HTLV-III Virus Exposure.* Atlanta: Centers for Disease Control (February).

———. 1986. "Acquired Immunodeficiency Syndrome (AIDS) among Blacks and Hispanics—United States." *Morbidity and Mortality Weekly Report (MMWR)* 35(October 24): 655–66.

———. 1987a. "Antibody to Human Immunodeficiency Virus in Female Prostitutes." *Morbidity and Mortality Weekly Report (MMWR)* 36(March 27): 157–61.

———. 1987b. Unpublished data. Telephone conversation with Mary Chamberlin, March.

———. 1988. *Acquired Immunodeficiency Syndrome (AIDS) Weekly Surveillance Report* (January 4).

Coates, Thomas J. 1985. "The Impact of AIDS on the Sexual Behavior of Gay Men." *Public Health Grand Rounds.* Sacramento, California: Department of Health Services.

Des Jarlais, D.C., et al. 1984. "Heterosexual Partners: A Large Risk Group for AIDS." *Lancet* 2(December 8):1346–47.

Mondanaro, J. 1981a. "Medical Services for Drug Dependent Women." In *Treatment Services for Drug Dependent Women,* vol. 1, edited by G.M. Beschner, B.G. Reed, and J. Mondanaro. Rockville, Maryland: National Institute on Drug Abuse, DHHS Publ. No. (ADM) 81-1177.

———. 1981b. "Reproductive Health Concerns for the Treatment of Drug Dependent Women." In *Treatment Services for Drug Dependent Women.* Vol. 1. *See* Mondanaro 1981a.

Mondanaro, J., et al. 1982. "Sexuality and Fear of Intimacy as Barriers to Recovery for Drug Dependent Women." In *Treatment Services for Drug Dependent Women.* vol. 2, edited by B.G. Reed, G.M. Beschner, and J.

Mondanaro. Rockville, Maryland: National Institute on Drug Abuse, DHHS Publ. No. (ADM) 82-1219.

Reed, Beth Glover. 1981. "Intervention Strategies for Drug Dependent Women: An Introduction." In *Treatment Services for Drug Dependent Women*. Vol. 1. *See* Mondanaro, 1981a.

Sandelowski, Margarette. 1981. *Women, Health, and Choice*. Englewood Cliffs, New Jersey: Prentice-Hall, Inc.

Shaw, Nancy S. 1985. "California Models for Women's AIDS Education and Services." Paper presented at the American Public Health Association Annual Meeting, Washington, D.C., November 20.

Sutker, Patricia B. 1981. "Drug Dependent Women: An Overview of the Literature. In *Treatment Services for Drug Dependent Women*. Vol. 1. *See* Mondanaro 1981a.

Wilsnack, Sharon C., and Linda J. Beckman, eds. 1984. *Alcohol Problems in Women*. New York: The Guilford Press.

Chapter 5

American Psychiatric Association. 1980. *Diagnostic and Statistical Manual of Mental Disorders*. 3d ed. Washington, D.C.: The American Psychiatric Association.

Bellantuono, C., et al. 1980. "Benzodiazepines: Clinical Pharmacology and Therapeutic Use." *Drugs* 19(March):195–219.

Friedel, Robert O. 1985. "Use of Anxiolytics: Prescribing Practices." In *Internal Medicine for the Specialist: Anxiolytic Evolution in Today's Anxious World*. Long Beach, California: Mead Publishing.

Greenblatt, D.J., et al. 1983. "Drug Therapy: Current Status of Benzodiazepines." Parts 1,2. *The New England Journal of Medicine* 309(Aug 11):354–358, Aug 18 410–416.

Kales, A., et al. 1982. "The Prescription of Hypnotic Drugs." In *Frequently Prescribed and Abused Drugs*, edited by Cohen S. et al. New York: The Haworth Press, Inc.

Kales, A., and J.D. Kales. 1984. *Evaluation and Treatment of Insomnia*. New York City, Oxford University Press.

Klerman, G.L. 1985. "Understanding Anxiety: Normal Emotion, Symptom, and Clinical Disorder. In *Internal Medicine for the Specialist*. *See* Friedel 1985.

Lader, Malcolm. 1985a. "Achieving Treatment Goals: Limitations of Therapies." In *Internal Medicine for the Specialist*. *See* Friedel 1985.

———. 1985b. "The Patient and Dependence." In *Internal Medicine for the Specialist*. *See* Friedel 1985.

Parry, H.J., et al. 1972. "National Patterns of Psychotherapeutic Drug Use." *Archives of General Psychiatry* 28(December):769.

Radcliffe, A., et al. 1985. *The Pharmer's Almanac: Pharmacology of Drugs*. Denver: M.A.C.

Rickels, K. 1985. "Overview." In *Symposium Highlights Anxiety Disorders: An*

International Update. New York City: Academy Professional Information Services, Inc.

Skegg, D.C.G., et al. 1977. "Use of Medicines in General Practice." *British Medical Journal* 2(June 18):1561–1563.

Swonger, A.K., and L.L. Constantine. 1983. *Drugs and Therapy: A Handbook of Psychotropic Drugs.* 2d ed. Boston: Little, Brown and Company.

Chapter 6

American Psychiatric Association. 1980. *Diagnostic and Statistical Manual of Mental Disorders Third Edition* Washington D.C.: The American Psychiatric Association.

American Psychiatric Association. 1987. *Diagnostic and Statistical Manual of Mental Disorders, Third Edition, Revised.* Washington, D.C.: The American Psychiatric Association.

Bem, S.L. 1974. "The Measurement of Psychological Androgyny." *Journal of Consulting and Clinical Psychology* 42(April):155–62.

Boskind-White, Marlene, and William White. 1983. *Bulimerexia.* New York City: W.W. Norton.

———. 1986. "Bulimerexia: A Historical-Sociological Perspective." In *Handbook of Eating Disorders,* edited by K. Brownell and J. Forcyt. New York: Basic Books.

Garfinkel, P., and A. Kaplan. 1986. "Anorexia Nervosa: Diagnostic Conceptualizations. In *Handbook of Eating Disorders. See* Boskind-White and White 1986.

Garner, David M., and Paul E. Garfinkel, eds. 1985. *Handbook of Psychotherapy for Anorexia Nervosa and Bulimia.* New York City: The Guilford Press.

Gomberg, E.L., and J.M. Lisansky. 1984. "Antecedents of Alcohol Problems in Women." In *Alcohol Problems in Women,* edited by S.C. Wilsnack and L.J. Beckman. New York: The Guilford Press.

Kaplan, A. 1986. "The 'Self-in-Relation': Implications for Depression in Women." *Psychotherapy* 23(Summer):234–242.

Martin, R.L., R.C. Cloninger, and S.B. Guze. 1985. "Alcohol Misuse and Depression in Women Criminals." *Journal of Studies on Alcohol* 46(January):65–71.

Neuman, P. and P. Halvorson. 1983. *Anorexia Nervosa and Bulimia: A Handbook for Counselors and Therapists.* New York City: Van Nostrand Reinhold.

Rybicki, D. 1986. "Problems with Addiction Model in Treatment." In *Eating Disorders Digest,* edited by Jan Wilson. Louisiana: Center Publishing.

Sheehan, David V. 1983. *The Anxiety Disease.* New York City: Charles Scribner's Sons.

Tinsley, E.G., S. Sullivan-Guest, and J. McGuire. 1984. "Feminine Sex Role and Depression in Middle-Aged Women." *Sex Roles* 11(July):25–32.

Weissman, M.M., and G.L. Klerman. 1982. "Sex Differences and the Epidemiology of Depression." In *Major Psychiatric Disorders: Overview and Selected Readings,* edited by F.G. Guggenheim and C. Nadelson. New York: Elsevier.

Chapter 7

800-COCAINE Hotline 1985 Telephone Conversation.

Byck, R., ed. 1974. *Cocaine Papers: Sigmund Freud.* New York City: Stonehill.

Johanson, C.E. et al. 1984. "Assessment of the Dependence Potential of Cocaine in Animals." In *Cocaine: Pharmacology, Effects and Treatment of Abuse.* J.G. Grabowski. National Institute on Drug Abuse Research Monograph 50 DHHS Publication Number (ADM) 84–1326. Washington, D.C.: Superintendent of Documents, U.S. Government Printing Office: 54–71.

Jones, E. 1961. *The Life and Work of Sigmund Freud.* Vol. 1. New York: Basic Books.

NIDA. 1986. *Executive Summary, Community Epidemiology Work Group.* Rockville, Maryland: National Institute on Drug Abuse (NIDA).

———. 1987. "Drug Abuse Warning Network (DAWN) Medical Examiner Data File." Unpublished five-year panel, National Institute on Drug Abuse (NIDA), Rockville, Maryland.

Smith, D.E. 1986. "Cocaine-Alcohol Abuse: Epidemiological, Diagnostic, and Treatment Considerations." *Journal of Psychoactive Drugs* 18(April–June):117–29.

Vereby, K., and M.S. Gold. 1984. "The Psychopharmacology of Cocaine." *Psychiatric Annals* 14(October):714–23.

Weil, A. 1983. *From Chocolate to Morphine: Understanding Mind Active Drugs.* Boston, Massachusetts: Houghton Mifflin.

Woods, J.H., and D.A. Downs. 1973. "The Psychopharmacology of Cocaine." In *Drug Use in America: Problem in Perspective, Appendix Volume I: Patterns and Consequences of Drug Use.* Washington, D.C.: U.S. Government Printing Office.

Recommended Reading

Chapter 2

Books

Black, Claudia. *Repeat After Me*. Denver: M.A.C., 1985.

Fossum, Merle A., and Marilyn J. Mason. *Facing Shame: Families in Recovery*. New York: W.W. Norton & Co., 1986.

Gravitz, Herbert L., and Julie D. Bowden. *Guide to Recovery: A Book for Adult Children of Alcoholics*. Holmes Beach, Florida: Learning Publications, 1985.

Schaff-Wilson, Ann. *Co-Dependence: Misunderstood—Mistreated*. San Francisco: Winston Press, 1986.

Shainess, Natalie. *Sweet Suffering: Woman as Victim*. New York City, New York: Bobbs-Merrill, 1984.

Chapter 3

Books

Abel, Ernest L. *Narcotics and Reproduction, a Bibliography*. Westport, Connecticut: Greenwood Press, 1983.

———. *Alcohol and Reproduction, a Bibliography*. Westport, Connecticut: Greenwood Press, 1983.

Ostrea, Enrique M., Cleofe J. Chavez, and Joan Stryker. *The Care of the Drug Dependent Woman and Her Infant*. Lansing, Michigan: Michigan Department of Public Health, 1979.

Articles and Reports

Anderson S.C. & Grant. "Pregnant Women and Alcohol: Implications to Social Work." *Social Casework* 65(January 1984):3.

Arena, J.M. "Drugs and Chemical Excreted in Breast Milk." *Pediatric Annals* 9(Dec. 1980):452–57.

Barrison, I.G. et al. "Screening for Alcohol Abuse in Pregnancy." *British Medical Journal* 285(November 6, 1982):1318.

Berlin, C.M. "The Excretion of Drugs in Human Milk." In *Drugs and Chemical Risks to the Fetus and Newborn, Progress in Clinical and Biological Research,* vol. 36, edited by R.H. Schwartz and S.J. Yaffe. New York: Alan R. Liss, 1980.

Boon, W.H. "Effects of Herbs and Drugs During Pregnancy and Lactation." *Journal of the Singapore Pediatric Society* 21(Sept.-Dec. 1979):169–78.

Clarren, S. "Recognition of Fetal Alcohol Syndrome." *Journal of American Medical Association.* 245(June 19, 1981):2436–2439.

Cohen, F.S., and J.D. Densen-Gerber. "A Study of the Relationship between Child Abuse and Drug Addiction in 178 Patients: Preliminary Results." *Child Abuse and Neglect* 6(? 1982):383–87.

Davidson, S., L. Alden, and P. Davison. "Changes in Alcohol Consumption after Childbirth." *Journal of Advanced Nursing* 6(May 1981):195–98.

Findlay, J.W.A., et al. "Analgesic Drugs in Breast Milk and Plasma." *Clinical Pharmacology and Therapeutics* 29(March 1981):625–33.

Fried, P.A. "Changing Patterns of Soft Drug Use Prior to and During Pregnancy: A Prospective Study." *Drug Alcohol Dependence* 6(November 1980):323–43.

Giacoia, G.P., and C.S. Catz. "Drugs and Pollutants in Breast Milk." *Clinics of Perinatology* 6(March 1979):181–99.

Harlap, S., and P.H. Shiono. "Alcohol, Smoking, and Incidence of Spontaneous Abortions in the First and Second Trimester." *Lancet* 2(July 26, 1980):173–76.

Hingson, R. "Effects of Maternal Drinking and Marijuana Use on Fetal Growth and Development." *Pediatrics* 70(October 1982):539–46.

Kautman, K.R., et al. "Phencyclidine in Umbilical Cord Blood: Preliminary Data." *American Journal of Psychiatry* 140(April 1983):452–54.

Kline, J., et al. "Drinking During Pregnancy and Spontaneous Abortion." *Lancet* 2(July 26, 1980):176–80.

Lawson, M.S., and G.S. Wilson. "Parenting among Women Addicted to Narcotics." *Child Welfare* 59(Feb. 1980):67–79.

Little, R.E. et al. "Public Awareness and Knowledge about the Risks of Drinking During Pregnancy in Multnomah, Oregon." *American Journal of Public Health* 71(March 1981):312–14.

May, P.A., and K.J. Hymbaugh. "A Pilot Project on Fetal Alcohol Syndrome among American Indians." *Alcohol Health and Research World* 7(Winter 1982–83):3–9.

Rosett, H.L. et al. "Patterns of Alcohol Consumption and Fetal Development." *Obstetrics and Gynecology* 61(May 1983):539–46.

Russell, M. "Drinking and Pregnancy: Review of Current Research." *NY State Journal of Medicine* 82(July 1982):1218–21.

Singh, R.K. "Experience with Pregnant Problem Drinkers" (letter). *Journal of American Medical Association* 250(November 4, 1983):2287.

Staisey, N.L., et al. "Relationship between Moderate Maternal Alcohol Consumption During Pregnancy and Infant Neurological Development." *Journal of Studies on Alcohol* 44(March 1983):262–70.

Steer, R.A., and J. Schut. "Moods of Pregnant and Nonpregnant Heroin Addicts." *The International Journal of the Addictions* 15(Nov. 1980):1279–83.

————. Stimmel, B. ed. "Effects of Maternal Alcohol and Drug Abuse on the Newborn." *Advances in Alcohol and Substance Abuse* 1(Spring–Summer 1982):1–145.

Strauss, A., et al. "Neonatal Manifestations of Maternal Phencyclidine (PCP) Abuse." *Pediatrics* 68(October 1981):550–52.

Streissguth, A.P. "Alcohol and Pregnancy, an Overview and an Update." *Substance Alcohol Actions Misuse* 4(1983):149–73.

U.S. Senate. "Effects of Alcohol Consumption During Pregnancy: Hearing Before the Subcommittee on Alcoholism and Drug Abuse of the Committee on Labor and Human Resources." Washington, D.C.: U.S. Government Printing Office, Document No. 99-9660, September 21, 1982.

Wallisch, D.K., and M.R. Steinberg. "Parenting Attitudes of Addict Mothers." *The International Journal of the Addictions* 15(1980):809–19.

Wilson, G.S., M.M. Desmond, and R.B. Wait. "Follow-up of Methadone-Treated and Untreated Narcotic-Dependent Women and Their Infants: Health, Developmental, and Social Implications." *The Journal of Pediatrics* 98 (1981):716–22.

Resources

The film *Condom Sense* was produced by the California Health Services Department, Office of Family Planning, in 1981. It is distributed by:

Perennial Films
930 Pitner Avenue
Evanston, IL 60202
(800) 323-9084

You can also contact local Planned Parenthood offices about the distribution of this film.

COYOTE organization for women in the sex industry:

P.O. Box 6297
San Francisco, CA 94101–6297
(415) 558-0450

A catalog of educational materials, sensitively prepared for high-risk groups, including women at risk and drug users, is available from:

San Francisco AIDS Foundation
The Women's Program
333 Valencia Street, Fourth Floor
San Francisco, CA 94103
(415) 864-4376
Hot line: (415) 863-AIDS

Index

About the Author

D r. **Josette Mondanaro** is a physician who has specialized in women's health and chemical dependency for twenty years. She has worked arduously as a clinician, administrator, writer, and educator to enhance the health and well-being of women and families. Currently Dr. Mondanaro is the director of a national AIDS prevention project for women, the Women and AIDS Risk Network or WARN.

A pioneer in women's health, Dr. Mondanaro designed and founded numerous women's clinics including: The Haight Ashbury Women's Clinic, The Ching Nin Asian Women's Clinic, The San Francisco Pregnant Addicts Program, The Marin Pregnant Addicts Program, and Wingspread: Comprehensive Health Services for Women.

In addition, Dr. Mondanaro has served as the Director of Substance Abuse for the State of California. She has written about chemical dependency and women's health in eighteen published articles and three books.

Dr. Mondanaro designed and teaches female physiology and gynecology as well as current issues in public health for the University of California at Santa Cruz.

In the past, Dr. Mondanaro served on the Executive Board of the California Society for the Treatment of Alcoholism and Other Drug Dependencies. She also served on the Physician Diversion Evaluation Committee and as a member of the Physician Peer Review Panel for the Board of Medical Quality Assurance.

Dr. Mondanaro is featured on four films: *Women, Drugs and Alcohol; One For My Baby,* a film about the fetal alcohol syndrome: *Treating the Chemically Dependent Woman and Her Child;* and *Innocent Addicts.* She has appeared on the Phil Donahue Show, Hour Magazine, Women to Women, NBC Nightly News with Tom Brokaw and Showtime's What's up America. *Ms.* Magazine, *Vogue,* and *Bride* have published interviews with this dynamic and dedicated physician.

DATE DUE